How to Be the Adult in the Room

in Life,

in Marriage,

as a Parent

by James Kelly

Ideas into Books®
WESTVIEW
KINGSTON SPRINGS, TENNESSEE

Ideas into Books®
W E S T V I E W
P.O. Box 605
Kingston Springs, TN 37082
www.publishedbywestview.com

ISBN 978-1-62880-030-2

First edition, April 2014
●

Table of Contents

Preface

I suppose one might consider me presumptive to write a book on how to be an adult. But on the contrary, I come to this rather intimidating subject with more of a sense of vulnerability. *How to be the Adult in the Room* is my first attempt at serious writing on this scale, and I realized, early on, I could not write this book without weaving threads of my own personal story into its fabric. I am, therefore, compelled to provide glimpses of my maturational journey and experiences that have shaped me and brought me to this endeavor.

I have worked as a psychotherapist in private practice now for over twenty-five years. I was originally attracted to the helping professions during my college days in Texas when I worked for an organization that provided group home care for foster children. I went on to work in the field of residential treatment with children and adolescents for approximately ten years during a journey that took me to Tennessee, Virginia, and North Carolina and thought I'd found my vocational destination in the child welfare field. But as I moved up the ranks in organizations and became removed from meaningful contact with those we served, the responsibility of dealing with budgets, boards of directors, and other administrative functions dissatisfied me. Our journeys have a way of taking unpredictable turns while rendering discoveries about who we are. I soon found myself, in my thirties with a wife and a young child, disillusioned with my career and lost in terms of my direction.

I retreated to the safety of a third generation family hardware business in Houston to sell nuts and bolts alongside my brother and father. I grew up working in the hardware store, and my familiarity with it made for a smooth transition. The security of the business and the support of having family nearby offered a soft place to land while my wife Catherine and I had our second child and sorted out our life. On a deeper level, however, I was grieving the loss of a sense of who I was and a loss of purpose and direction. I also felt out of place in Houston, despite having grown up there. I'd become strongly attached to the southeastern part of the country, where we had lived for years, so was also experiencing a loss of place.

I suppressed this internal conflict for the sake of family stability, but about five years into our life in Houston, my feelings began to force their way to the surface in the form of classic symptoms of anxiety. My body was telling me, on many levels, I was not where I belonged. In grappling with all of this more consciously, two main realizations became clear: First, I needed to re-enter the helping profession and more specifically as a clinician, not an administrator. And, secondly, we needed to find our way back to the Southeast. In all of this I was blessed to have a patient and supportive wife, Catherine, who knew where I belonged vocationally and who also missed the Southeast.

I was overwhelmed at first as I considered, in my late thirties with two small children, uprooting and starting over, but Catherine and I felt in our hearts it was right. We chose Nashville where we were drawn to the natural beauty of Tennessee and had friends and professional connections.

There is a spiritual principle that says, when you find the right path, doors will open. Immediately upon our return to Nashville, through a contact with a past colleague, I was hired as a child and family therapist at a beginning level salary. This time around I knew I was building a career as a clinician. Then, just as I gained my footing as a therapist, two more doors opened. First, I landed a consulting and training contract with a statewide association of agencies serving foster children and soon after, a good friend invited me to join him and his associates in their counseling group, with my own practice. The contract work allowed me enough income and flexibility to take on the risk of private practice.

In the span of only three years, I went from helping manage Kelly's Hardware with my family in Texas to developing and delivering training in a field I loved while building a private counseling practice, one of my ultimate goals, in beautiful Tennessee.

Years earlier, in college, and confused about my direction, I took a career services assessment that revealed my best fits were in teaching and in the helping professions. Yet, it wasn't until my fortieth year that, for the first time, I was doing the work I was meant to do and living where I felt the most at home. The late Joseph Campbell, one of my many teachers, coined the term, "follow your bliss." That was what I was finally doing and my anxiety began to dissolve.

Now that I have been in private practice for twenty-five years, I have a desire for a new challenge: I want to capture in writing what I've learned and shared with clients throughout my career.

I've long considered putting pen to paper to recount my clients' stories of challenges and breakthroughs, along with my own human experience to illustrate the nature of life's developmental processes. It has taken every one of my thirty-five years as a professional helper, combined with my own personal journey, to fully integrate theory and experience. This is a labor of love for the many clients who have asked for a book recommendation to reinforce their therapy. Just as my clinical work aims at helping people grow, my genuine desire is for *How to be the Adult in the Room* to foster growth in every reader.

Introduction

"I know of no more encouraging fact than the unquestionable ability of man to elevate his life by conscious endeavor."

~Henry David Thoreau

Most of what I think I know, my clients have taught me. When you sit with people several hours a day, most days of the week, for many years, as they confide their darkest secrets and deepest pain, you become transformed. You learn to listen and observe on a unique frequency and gain access to a heightened level of insight into the human experience.

As you sharpen these listening skills and hear more stories, you begin to recognize the common threads that run through the stories. They are diverse and the detail is unique, but the larger themes and patterns repeat themselves over and over. There is an abundance of self-help literature that has captured these insights and has empowered millions of people. These authors have popularized concepts that would otherwise be beyond most people's grasp. For example, there is a growing common knowledge of frameworks such as dysfunctional families, co-dependency, the child within, learned survival roles, stages of grief, boundaries, inner dialogue, negative programs, love languages, higher consciousness and many more. It is an ever-expanding list. I hope to bring to common awareness one more – the adult in the room.

There are also a variety of approaches to therapy. These modes have names such as experiential, client-centered, play therapy, art and music therapy, family therapy, group therapy, hypnotherapy, behavior therapy, and cognitive therapy, just to name a few. There, too, is the medical model approach that emphasizes the use of medication. All of these approaches have merit and have helped countless people.

Every therapist draws on elements from a variety of modes, but eventually narrows his or her approach down to two or three with which one is most compatible and uses predominantly. I, too, integrate a variety of elements, but my dominant approach is what is commonly known as cognitive therapy. The premise of cognitive therapy is that the quality of one's life is largely determined by one's thoughts and beliefs, meaning one's happiness is influenced less by the circumstances of life and more by the interpretation of the circumstances. For example, someone with a powerful underlying and often unconscious core belief that tells him "I'm not good enough" can be tormented by some type of rejection either real or perceived, because it serves to confirm his inferiority. Many people live in these distorted worlds, accounting for most anxiety and depression. On the other hand, someone else who has a core belief that tells him "I'm acceptable as I am" and experiences some type of rejection may feel hurt and disappointed, but recovers quickly because it doesn't threaten his positive belief about himself.

Cognitive therapy helps people connect the dots by helping them consciously trace many of their negative emotions to certain triggers that activate a mental process of interpreting or perceiving through self-talk or visual images. This is all based on powerful and oftentimes unconscious, distorted core beliefs. Therapy also exposes how the distorted beliefs formed, usually from stressful childhood experiences.

When one begins to develop this new insight and awareness, he can then begin to practice new thinking skills. When he encounters a trigger that sends him reeling, he can catch it, as it is happening, and consciously give it meaning based on reality with more reassuring self-talk. The result is either more positive feelings or minimized negative impacts. Consider the woman who, as a child, was continually criticized by her parents. No matter what she did, even if it was positive, they would focus on how it could be better. As a result, she internalized a core belief that said, "I'm not good enough;" "I have to be perfect." When she makes honest mistakes at work, she's devastated. When she achieves something impressive, she cannot enjoy it because she feels it could have been better. She struggles with anxiety and depression. In therapy, she becomes aware of the self-critical inner-dialogue that is triggered by a simple mistake. She learns how to interrupt this negative self-talk and to practice reminding herself to be human is to make mistakes and to learn from them. She also learns to remind herself she doesn't have to be perfect, because there is no such thing as perfect. She learns to take her mistakes in stride.

By now, you may be asking what cognitive therapy has to do with being the adult in the room. The short answer is adult behavior is not instinctive, whereas childish behavior is. Adult behavior requires the ability to process life at a high level of consciousness in order to apply the kind of insights and thinking skills that equip us to override our defensive instincts. In my work, I've witnessed how the learning and practice of these skills can accelerate one's growth and maturity. I will address, in this book, the specifics of these skills.

One key way I frame my view of humans is we are truly works in progress and all in some stage of maturational development. In fact, we have two ages: a chronological age and a developmental age. Often, our chronological age does not reflect where we are developmentally or maturationally. Some people exhibit maturity beyond their years, but too often we see what appear to be children in grown-up bodies. Due to my work, I understand why many people get stuck in their development; so, in some ways I'm helping grown-ups learn how to be adults. In my experience, people who have the courage to come to therapy are the ones who are taking responsibility for themselves through self-examination and new learning. In *How to Be the Adult in the Room*, I'm writing to people who may not seek counseling but would pick up a book, and also are eager for change through self-examination.

Because I'm developmentally oriented, I can't help but look at the behavior of grown-ups without registering whether it reflects the actions of a child or an adult. As I look around, it seems as though I see too many children in grown-up bodies. I must be watching too many T.V. reality shows, because it is as if our culture has embraced adolescence as the model for behavior. I do have serious concern about what our culture, through media, is teaching people about adulthood. Likewise, when I see us, in this digital age, becoming more systematically and unconsciously oriented to external stimuli and less introspective and reflective, I worry that real adults may be an endangered species.

My purpose in this book is first to raise awareness of an important and universal human issue. And secondly, to take what is truly a complex issue and make it so understandable and practical that anyone committed to his or her personal growth can apply it.

Before I tackle this challenge, I must issue a few qualifications. This book assimilates many insights I've gained from working on the front lines with people in my practice. This book is not intended to be an academic treatise. I'm sure human development scholars might find a thing or two to challenge. There is nothing in this book that claims to be absolute. There are always exceptions to rules. Trust yourself and make your own decisions regarding what is useful to you. Everything in these pages has been said in thousands of ways over thousands of years. *How to Be the Adult in the Room* simply applies a developmental frame to long-held truths.

The examples I use to develop the upcoming topics are composite pictures drawn from the many personal stories I've heard over the years. Likewise, the names I use are fictional. Finally, I'm going to use the term "children in grown-up bodies" many times in the following pages. I want to emphasize that my use of this term is in no way derogatory. When I think of "children in grown-up bodies," it evokes compassion in me, because I witness how distressing it can be for people to try to function in the adult world without adults tools. We all are subject, at times, to thinking, feeling, and behaving childishly. My intention in using this term is to gently confront all of us – me included – in order to raise our awareness of aspects of our own immaturity and to challenge us to strive, when it really counts, to be the adult in the room.

One: The Adult in Life

The Traits of the Adult

Trying to define adulthood is like trying to define "human being" or "happiness". You can get in the ballpark and you can describe elements, but there is no way to completely pin it down. Years ago when I began to frame my work in terms of helping people grow, I created a handout, displayed ahead, attempting to describe for clients what I identified as the key contrasts between child and adult that have nothing to do with age. These traits represent extreme points on a continuum, meaning a person can be on one extreme end or the other or fall somewhere in the middle. There are degrees of maturity and immaturity. I've used this handout to help clients self-assess and to provide definition to the goal of developing the traits of the adult.

I've come to the conclusion that adulthood is not a constant state we achieve and, upon arrival, sustain naturally. I believe being the adult reflects a state of consciousness that empowers us to choose learned insights, thoughts, beliefs, perceptions, and learned interpersonal skills when processing everyday life experience and responding to it. The adult has developed the ability to maintain this state of consciousness with fair consistency. No one can do this perfectly. Because we are flawed human beings and have powerful survival instincts and needs, we all regress. On a bad day, given the right circumstances, I can be the child in the grown-up body. It is really a question of frequency and degree.

To the casual observer, there appear to be puzzling contradictions. For example, it is not unusual for me to see someone who functions consistently as an adult at work, but seems to function too much like a child in her marriage or in relating to her own children. This suggests there are unconscious barriers that need to be identified and resolved before progress can be made.

Becoming the adult is a challenge. It requires a conscious choice to learn and grow. Human growth is slow, subtle, incremental, and hard to measure in short periods of time. Human growth is non-linear. Progress is made by taking two steps forward and one step back, but the rewards are great.

I often advise clients to use a graph of the stock market as a metaphor for understanding how human change and growth occurs. I explain to them the quick fix is a myth and real progress can only be made through the process of learning new insights and skills. The integration of this new learning requires time, patience, practice, and perseverance. With rare exceptions, when one is trying to make changes in life, it is unrealistic to expect marked results in a few weeks or even months. Rather than expect something dramatic, I teach people how to spot the small signs of progress that keep them encouraged. For example, someone who is working on being more assertive might report she failed to take advantage of an opportunity to practice assertiveness recently. I point out that her awareness that it was a missed opportunity is an important step compared to her lack of awareness three months ago.

As you read this book, I want you to avoid thinking in quick-fix terms – what has to change now. Think in big picture and slow growth terms – what you want your life to be like a year from now, five years from now, ten years from now. Know that if you practice the insights and skills identified in this book with patience and perseverance, you will continue to grow and mature and your life will be richer.

The handout I created for clients, displayed ahead, serves as an assessment tool and a guide. This list of traits also serves as an outline for much of this book. This list is not intended to be all-inclusive. We all have valid beliefs about what comprises maturity. I've targeted traits that relate to the most recurring barriers to adulthood I encounter in my clinical practice.

The Ten Traits of the Adult

The Child   **The Adult**

SELF-ACCEPTANCE

Has little or no formed   Has a well-developed
sense of self. Derives   sense of self with
self-worth from the   fundamental self-
approval of others.   acceptance.

1………..……2……………...3…………….....4…………...…5

INDEPENDENT THINKING

Is unable to validate one's   Believes in the validity of
own thoughts and   one's own thoughts and
feelings and takes cues   feelings and is guided by
from others.   one's own trusted thinking.

1………..……2……………...3…………….....4…………...…5

PERSONAL RESPONSIBILITY

Depends on others to   Accepts total
intuit and meet needs   responsibility for the
and blames others for   meeting of needs and the
unhappiness.   quality of life.

1………..……2……………...3…………….....4…………...…5

Conscious Feeling

Is often controlled by
feelings.

Processes and manages
feelings consciously.

1...........2.............3...........4...........5

Positive Core Beliefs

Is often controlled by
unconscious negative
thoughts and beliefs.

Often consciously
chooses thoughts and
beliefs that enhance the
quality of life.

1...........2.............3...........4...........5

Insight

Functions with little to no
insight and reacts
instinctively to what is on
the surface.

Has developed key
insights that equip one to
understand the
complexities in life and
respond constructively.

1...........2.............3...........4...........5

Assertiveness

Relies on control,
manipulation, and
defenses to communicate
thoughts and feelings and
to get needs met.

Has learned how to assert
thoughts, feelings, and
needs skillfully in order to
get needs met.

1...........2.............3...........4...........5

SACRIFICE

Is pre-occupied with
one's own needs and not
responsive to others'
needs.

Balances equally, making
sacrifices for the needs of
others and tending to
one's own valid needs.

1………..……..2……………....3…………….....4…………...…..5

COMPETENCE

Lacks the knowledge and
skills necessary to
function competently in
the adult world.

Has acquired the
knowledge and skills
necessary for satisfying
work, satisfying
relationships, and
independent living.

1………..……..2……………....3…………….....4…………...…..5

PERSONAL GROWTH

Is focused on safety and
is risk avoidant.

Values new learning and
growth and can take
emotional risks.

1………..……..2……………....3…………….....4…………...…..5

TRAIT ONE

Self-Acceptance

"This above all else: to thine own self be true."
~William Shakespeare

"Just trust yourself; then you will know how to live."
~Joann Wolfgang von Goethe

"Nothing can bring you peace but yourself."
~Ralph Waldo Emerson

"Nobody can make you feel inferior without your consent."
~Eleanor Roosevelt

"The Master understands that the universe
Is forever out of control and
Does not try to dominant events.
Because he believes in himself,
He does not try to convince others.
Because he is content with himself,
He does not need others' approval.
Because he accepts himself,
The whole world accepts him."

~Lao-tzu

Self-Acceptance

*I am developing a positive sense of who I am
with fundamental self-acceptance.*

Adam was in his late thirties and had experienced mild anxiety and depression as long as he could remember. We quickly connected these mood problems to his many insecurities. In one of our sessions, he described attending a recent dinner party during which he went from feeling good in the beginning, to noticing his mood shift in the middle, to feeling depressed toward the end of the evening. It wasn't difficult for us to connect the dots. At some point during the party the discussion among the men with whom he was surrounded turned to football – team analysis, specific players, statistics. He didn't have a clue what they were talking about much less any interest. This discussion was the trigger, but for what?

Adam grew up with a father and older brother whom he described as sports fanatics. He was never interested in sports. From an early age he was drawn to music and other creative activities. Adam always felt that his lack of interest in sports disappointed his father and was the main barrier to a closer relationship with him. He was realizing he had internalized a belief, when he was a young boy, that something must be wrong with him since he was not athletic and had no interest in sports.

It was an epiphany for him to see how an innocent conversation could activate this still powerful unconscious insecurity in him. We agreed it was time in his life to accept himself as a man whose interests didn't include sports. This was but one of many perfectly acceptable aspects of who he was for which he doubted himself.

As I approach the issue of sense of self, I'm reminded of the movie *City Slickers* starring Billy Crystal and Jack Palance. Crystal plays an advertising salesman working in a New York City corporate office, approaching his fortieth birthday and a mid-life crisis. He has lost his passion for work and his sense of direction. In an attempt to find himself he signs up to be a trail hand on an authentic old west cattle drive where he meets a rough, grizzled trail boss played by Palance.

Once on the trail, Crystal confides his internal crisis to Palance, who stoically looks at Crystal, puffs on his hand-rolled cigarette, holds up one finger and says, "This is the secret to life." Crystal, puzzled, asks, "Your finger is the secret to life?" Palance responds, "The secret to life is one thing." Crystal with anticipation asks, "What's the one thing?" Palance replies, "That's what you have to figure out."

I've come to the conclusion the secret to life is found in the answer to the universal existential human question, "Who am I?" I can say with confidence most of our mental, emotional, and spiritual problems are symptomatic of our not knowing and trusting ourselves. Self-knowledge and self-trust provide an internal compass to guide you toward the purpose for which you were created. This compass leads you to the people and places that are right for you and away from what is not. Self-knowledge and self-trust provide the inner security needed to sustain you through the tough times. Without this grounding, life's challenges can be immobilizing and even small stresses can be overwhelming.

How would you answer the question, "Who are you?" Would you describe yourself physically? Would you emphasize what you do vocationally? Would you stress the roles you play, like wife and mother or husband and father? Would you focus on the groups you belong to? Would you judge yourself for not being who you think you should be?

Those answers, of course, reveal some important things about your life; but, in order to develop a strong sense of who you are, the answers have to go deeper. The depth of the answers reveals the depth of your self-knowledge. We have to have lived long enough, to have enough life experience, and to have been tested enough in order to consolidate an accurate sense of who we are. Even then, we will always be works in progress.

It is my view, the decade of our twenties is the period when we are most actively and consciously discovering who we are. In fact, recent results of a long-term National Institute of Health study have confirmed the human brain is not fully wired until our mid-twenties, meaning adolescent immaturity extends well into our third decade. It is in our twenties when we are forced to think about and make decisions for the future. This requires us to discover more about our own priorities, our true interests, our natural abilities, our unique personality traits, our true values and beliefs, and our life purpose and direction. The answers to these questions hold the keys to defining who we are. People who have explored these questions in depth and have found true answers are the ones who possess a strong sense of self. Those who have not reflected enough or have gone the path of least resistance are usually left with a shallow and superficial sense of self.

When I went to college, I had little understanding of who I was. I knew even less about what I wanted to do with my future. By default, I chose to major in business, since it was the only life I knew, having grown up in a family hardware business. I was so busy having fun it didn't dawn on me until the end of my third year that I was close to getting a degree in a field in which I'd never become particularly interested. I remember the pivotal moment as if it was yesterday. I was sitting in my statistics class and a wave of panic swept over me. My inner voice was shouting: "What are you doing here?" I suppressed the impulse to run out of the room, but left with a sense of urgency to seek answers for what I was truly meant to do with my life. In many ways it was the defining moment in my life. It would have been easy, in the short-term, to finish my business degree and make the best of it. Fortunately, I was determined to find deeper answers and put myself through a battery of assessments offered by the Career Services Department. The feedback from that process was clear that my best matches were in teaching and in the helping professions. I can still remember the resonance I felt when I read the report. That process helped sharpen my awareness of other parts of who I am – my personality, abilities, and values. Perhaps the turning point for me in that process was how much more consciously I began to listen to and to trust myself – a thread that has run through my life ever since. Adults have learned to locate and to trust their true inner voice that informs them of who they really are, whereas children in grown-up bodies are still listening to outside voices to be who the world expects them to be.

Developing a positive sense of self requires a conscious effort to reflect on deeper questions about who you are. With this true, authentic sense of who you are comes gut-level, feel-it-in-your-bones self-acceptance – the cornerstone of being the adult in the room. This kind of self-acceptance is transcendent of ego. It is a spiritual understanding of your divine nature and worth as a human being.

Our culture programs us to believe self-worth is to be measured and achieved. It orients us to compare ourselves to others according to our appearance, status, material, intelligence, and personality. It tells us how we *should* think and feel and be in order to gain approval. This programming is insidious as to how powerfully it orients us to the external world.

Abraham Maslow, the renowned developmental psychologist, once said, "The self-actualized person has become independent of the good opinion of other people." This is an elegant way of saying the adult in the room has outgrown comparing himself to, competing with, and needing the approval of the others in the room. The adult is aware there is no such reality as one person being more worthy than another, no matter our differences. The adult view is we humans are all in the same boat: flawed, limited, and imperfect, yet all with inherent redeeming value. We all share a common human experience in that we all know pain of some kind. Each of us has our own experience with fear and insecurity, and with loss and grief that binds us as a human family. The adult does not compute thoughts like "something is wrong with me," "I'm not good enough," or "I don't belong."

Make no mistake: I'm not talking about something simple. People who, in childhood, experienced abuse, neglect, trauma, rejection, and loss, or grew up in a generally unhealthy environment, likely internalized powerful negative core beliefs that present real barriers to self-acceptance. Psychotherapy is a means to help people heal the damage done by these experiences and guide them on a path to self-acceptance. The challenge is not limited to victims of abuse and neglect. Developing true self-acceptance is a universal human challenge. The good news is, with conscious practice, self-acceptance is within everyone's reach.

In the privacy of my office, highly successful people regularly admit deep insecurities, which rob them of peace and happiness. In fact, in many cases their achievements are driven by the desire to prove themselves. Yet, their achievements never satisfy the deeper need to feel whole for just being who they are. Here are examples of how lack of self-acceptance sounds when people reject aspects of who they are:

- I should be more logical and less emotional.
- I should be more outgoing and social.
- I'm not creative enough.
- I'm too soft-hearted.
- I should be more driven and goal-oriented.
- I should want to read more than I do.
- I'm too serious and not funny enough.

The adult can answer, with substance, what she's come to know and trust about herself and what thoughts and beliefs guide her.

When I work on this issue with clients, I help them identify aspects of who they are in the following areas:

- Inherent personality traits
- Natural abilities
- True interests
- True values and principles
- True thoughts and feelings

This process requires them to practice orienting internally. Self-acceptance brings an empowering inner security that dissolves certain fears and anxieties. There is no need for self-protective vigilance, because there's nothing in the room that has the power to threaten. There are only other flawed human beings in the room. Insecurity is replaced with an inner calm and new positive energy, which attracts what we want. When we remove our preoccupation with our inadequacies and what other people think, we're more authentic, spontaneous and playful. With self-acceptance, a setback is not a confirmation of defectiveness; it is the human experience to endure, deal with, and learn from.

Here are examples of how self-acceptance sounds:

- I'm not the most creative person, but I'm good at organizing the task.
- My family loves sports, but I love music and writing.
- I'm more of an introvert, so I like socializing with just a few people.
- I'm a very logical person, so sometimes I can be a little insensitive.
- I'm a fairly driven person, so I have to learn how to stop and smell the roses.

Deborah was in her mid-twenties and struggled with chronic anxiety and anorexia – a very complex issue. In my experience, anorexia is usually symptomatic of a few predictable themes – perfectionism, achievement, and control, though what I typically find at the heart of the problem is an undeveloped sense of self.

This young woman, who was a nurse, exhibited these patterns. Her compliant personality oriented her as a child to take her cues from other people and to try to please them. Her parents divorced when she was young, and she lost close contact with her father. She grew up longing to feel closer and more loved by her father, which undermined her self-worth. Her personality also predisposed her to strive to be in control. As she grew up, these factors coalesced to work against her. Along the way she became deeply insecure, and her maladaptive response was to try to be perfect to win outside approval and validation. She always made straight A's in school and graduated at the top of her nursing class. Yet, she never felt good enough. She was an excellent nurse, but constantly compared herself to peers and would look for evidence to find herself lacking. On the outside, she appeared to have it all together. On the inside, she was a train wreck. This is where anorexia came in. Like many women in our culture who feel insecure with themselves and out of control internally, she focused on controlling and perfecting her body to gain a sense of self-worth and control. The psychological reward gained by achieving this essentially unhealthy thinness is, of course, fleeting, illusory, and never satisfying.

The only real solution was for Deborah to decide that who she was had little to do with her body, her achievements, and the approval of others. While she was gaining an awareness of the elements of who she was, she had to learn how to accept, listen to, validate, be guided by, and trust her true self – not a simple process. She had to completely re-orient herself from taking cues from others to finding and trusting her own center. As she developed a more authentic sense of her own identity and learned to trust and accept herself, she began to feel more secure internally. This internal sense of control allowed her to start shedding, little by little, the need to be perfect. She began to accept her own flawed, limited, imperfect human nature, including her body. Her anxiety began to resolve as she was able to validate her own competency, stop comparing herself to the other nurses, and enjoy her work. Deborah must continue to practice this higher consciousness, but she's clearly on the path.

Helping people form a more positive sense of who they are is a slow step-by-step process. The following are some of the assignments I give to clients to help them on the path to self-knowledge, self-trust, and self-acceptance:

- Take a do-it-yourself version of an established personality trait assessment. I prefer the *Myers-Briggs Personality Inventory*. Make sure you get a thorough explanation of the results. I recommend a book entitled *Please Understand Me: Character and Temperament Types* by David Keirsey and Marilyn Bates.
- If you can afford it, take *The Highlands Ability Battery*, available at Highlandsco.com. This is an excellent natural ability assessment. Again, get a thorough interpretation of the results.
- Take time to identify and list as many of your true unique interests as you can.
- Practice identifying your own true values that you consciously choose, regardless of what other people think.
- Practice writing your own guiding principles and personal philosophy.
- Observe to what extent you try to read people's minds and take your cues from what others think and to what extent you do your own thinking.
- Ask yourself often, "What do I think?"
- Observe to what extent you compare yourself to others and what you tell yourself.
- Observe and listen to your feelings. Identify them, experience them, validate them, and figure out what your feelings are telling you.
- Create a written vision of what you want.
- Complete the sentence, "I am _____" twenty times without referring to your body or your appearance.

Using the scale from the "Ten Traits of the Adult," circle your
level of maturity related to the trait of self-acceptance. Then
identify a growth goal and one or more specific steps you will
begin to take.

You have little to no   You have a well-
positive sense of self and   developed sense of self
you derive self-worth   with fundamental self-
from the approval of   acceptance.
others.

1………..…….2……………....3…………....4………...….5

Growth goal:

Specific steps:

TRAIT TWO

Independent Thinking

"Do not believe what you have heard.
Do not believe in tradition because it is handed down many generations.
Do not believe in anything that has been spoken of many times.
Do not believe because the written statements come from an old sage.
Do not believe in conjecture.
Do not believe in authority or teachers or elders.
But after careful observations and analysis, when it agrees with reason and it
    will benefit one and all, then accept it and live by it."

~Buddha

"I do not feel obliged to believe that the same God who has endowed us with
sense, reason, and intellect has intended us to forego their use."

~Galileo

"To know what you prefer, instead of saying 'Amen' to what the world tells
you that you ought to prefer, is to keep your soul alive."

~Robert Louis Stevenson

Independent Thinking

I believe in the validity of my own thoughts,
and I am guided by my own trusted self-knowledge.

Lisa was a thirty-six-year-old woman in the process of ending her second marriage. She was questioning whether or not she was capable of a marriage commitment at all. What struck me most was that her primary concern was her mother's disapproval. When we got to deeper issues during her therapy, it became clear she didn't know who she was nor did she know and trust her own thinking. She was an obedient child raised by a controlling mother who told her what to think, feel, and be. Because of her compliant personality, she became so oriented to her mother's thinking and expectations, her sense of self and ability to think for herself never developed. Upon reflection, she realized she unconsciously chose her first husband out of rebellion; he represented many of the traits of which her mother disapproved. She unconsciously chose her second husband in order to please her mother; he possessed all of the qualities her mother liked. Of course, what was missing was her sense of what she really wanted and what was truly right for her. For thirty-six years, she'd taken her cues from others and didn't know how to think for herself. She began to see clearly how many of her problems stemmed from this core issue.

The seventeenth century French philosopher Rene Descartes said, "I think, therefore, I am." Nothing gives me more of a sense of who I am than when I know I'm doing my own thinking. When I work with a client toward the goal of developing a stronger sense of self, I emphasize that the degree to which we do our own thinking reflects how much our individual identify has formed. Most people don't do enough of their own thinking. Most of our thinking reflects what we are unconsciously programmed to think by our family, community, church, friends, the groups we join, and society at large. This is simply a fact of life. These influences can be either helpful or harmful, depending on how healthy they are. In either case, there is pressure to "follow the program." When we comply, we are rewarded with acceptance and approval. When we do not comply, there is usually a price to pay.

During my college years, I actively participated in a fraternity. I loved the experience and I made great friends. In my junior year I was elected vice-president of the fraternity. In mid-year, our pledge trainer unexpectedly resigned and, on short notice, I had to step into the role of pledge trainer. There had been a long tradition of trainers instilling the belief in pledges that we were the best fraternity on campus. I was uncomfortable with encouraging a group to believe they were better than other groups. Instead, I emphasized fraternities were equal in that each had its own personality, character, and strengths, and it was a matter of individuals and fraternities finding their match.

When it was time for new elections, I ran for president. On the night of the election, candidates stood before the membership to answer questions. Almost immediately an outspoken and influential member confronted me, wanting to know why I didn't teach pledges we were the best fraternity on campus. I said I couldn't promote something I didn't believe and explained my view. He made clear his opinion that I wasn't qualified to lead the fraternity with such weak loyalty. My losing the election may not have turned on that issue, but it seemed my leadership had been respected up to that point. In looking back, I remember being completely at peace with the election's outcome, and I can see this occurred at a time in my development when I was consolidating my sense of self by increasingly trusting my own thinking

Denise, a forty-year-old woman, felt guilty much of the time and was never at peace. She explained she grew up in a strict religious family with a steady diet of messages about what she *should* think and believe and what she *should* do as a good Christian. Denise went on to give an example of what she experienced. Her parents stressed she should never miss church unless she had an illness. She explained she'd worked overtime the previous week and stayed home from church Sunday morning, exhausted. She felt guilty and hoped God would forgive her since she was not technically sick.

So here was a forty-year-old woman who had never become oriented to trust her own thinking and decision-making. This may seem to be an extreme example to some people, but believe it or not, I see versions of this dynamic at work in peoples' lives on a regular basis in my practice.

I'm convinced one of the greatest gifts parents can give their children is encouragement to trust their own thinking. As Denise and I continued to explore the source of her guilt, it became obvious her orientation to what other people think dominated her life in every area. She often believed what she thought and felt was wrong. I heard her mistrust voiced in statements such as "I should think this way," or "I shouldn't feel that way." She carried this insecurity without awareness of how it undermined her peace and happiness every day of her life. She wanted to overcome the subsequent anxiety and depression caused by her over-orientation to what other people think.

When people are not oriented to their own thinking, teaching them how to think for themselves and trust their own thinking can be complicated. It is as if the circuitry in their brains has to be re-wired. So, I walk them through a step-by-step process.

- I first explain the rationale – true inner security, peace, and happiness are based on our trust in our own thinking and our own selves. Otherwise, we go through life attempting to read people's minds and taking our cues from what others think, which is a real roller-coaster ride.

- Secondly, I ask them to start observing how much mind reading they do and how oriented they are to what other people think and feel. They are often amazed at how much of this they are doing unconsciously. This step in consciousness activates a new circuit.

- I also ask them to listen for the self-talk that tells them things like, "What I think isn't important;" "Everyone knows more than I do;" I'm not smart enough;" and "People will disapprove of what I think." These self-critical, self-mistrusting voices need to be exposed and re-programmed. This consciousness activates another new circuit.

- Once they become fully aware of their hyper-vigilance to what others think and feel, and are aware of their self-talk, I ask them to practice asking two basic questions: "What do I think?" and "What is right for me?" Clients often tell me they draw a blank with these questions because they don't know what they think. I encourage them to persevere. It is like exercising an atrophied muscle. Little by little, answers will come.

- If they are in an individual conversation or a group discussion and they have an opinion about something, I encourage them to practice voicing it while telling themselves their thinking is valid.

- If they have an opportunity to state a preference about something or make a request of someone, I encourage them to do so as another way of practicing validating their own thinking.

Mature, independent thought starts by approaching most things with an open mind and the insight that life is complicated. Rarely are there simple answers when it comes to the human experience. Mature thinking carefully arrives at conclusions based on an internal deliberative process that considers different sides of an issue or question. Thinking that is starkly black and white, dogmatic, and self-righteous is defensive thinking based on fear, ignorance, and immaturity. On the other extreme are those who haven't formed opinions about much of anything. This too is an indication of immaturity. Adult thinking requires forming your own authentic set of beliefs, values, principles, and philosophies independent of family, friends, and culture. Mature thinking remains open to the influence of new information and new insight.

I'm going to claim some editorial license here and apply what I believe mature thinking looks like in the political arena. I'm writing this book at a time when it seems our political discourse is more polarized and destructive than I've ever witnessed. How honest conflict is approached, whether between individuals or entire groups of people, separates the children from the adults. In the political arena, we see a power struggle based on ideology. The children in grown-up bodies have to be right and have to win at all costs or they will "take their ball and go home." In the process, the child in the grown-up body will use inflammatory rhetoric and demonize his opponent to intimidate and to win. His paradigm is "win-lose". The adult in the room also has strong, principled beliefs, but he has the wisdom to understand ideological purity is a trap and each philosophy has some relevance. Therefore, he approaches conflict with a spirit of respect toward the other and a willingness to achieve a "win-win" through compromise – the only mature way to resolve conflict and to solve problems. I look to moderates as the adults in the political arena – those who look for the compromise and use their own judgment, rather than party loyalists who often practice groupthink. Sadly, moderates are sometimes marginalized, as some view compromise as disloyal. To solve problems at a high level, voters would do well to value independent thinking in those we elect.

Now, having referenced politics, I'm compelled to share my experience with religion as it relates to independent thinking. I once co-led a Sunday morning Bible study at a church I previously attended. My co-leader was a religion professor at a local university; he gave our duo biblical scholarship credibility. I facilitated the class discussion. I'd been in enough Sunday school classes in which a supposed authority interpreted scripture for me, so I agreed to lead the class on the condition we were allowed freedom to use our own approach. Bob and I set aside the denominational study guide and created our own simple format. We would decide, as a group, what book of the Bible to study and then, in each class, we would read a passage of scripture. Bob would provide historical context and I would ask the class what they thought. Once we knew and trusted each other enough to open up, it became an environment in which class members felt the freedom to question anything and to try out their own interpretations of what the scripture meant to them. It was the most meaningful church experience many of us had had thanks to the level of freedom and honesty achieved in that class. I'm convinced the support we felt to trust our own thinking fostered spiritual growth. My main complaint with many church cultures is the freedom to think independently is not cultivated, and in some churches clearly discouraged.

In my view, a mature religious faith has undergone some kind of deconstruction/reconstruction process through questioning and reflecting. This frees individuals to embrace beliefs that harmonize with their sense of self and truly enhance their quality of life. A mature faith puts emphasis on the empowering effects of its spiritual principles rather than on a defense of its doctrine. People who claim beliefs blindly and wholly, without question, are in some state of denial and not being honest with themselves. Not only is this an immature faith, it can be psychologically unhealthy too.

Tim, a college student who came to therapy reporting symptoms of anxiety, represents another example of how failing to think independently can manifest itself. Tim explained he was a pre-med major with a minor in psychology. On the surface, his stress was caused by his struggle with Biology and Chemistry classes. Physical sciences, he shared, were difficult for him, but he loved his psychology classes. I began to question why he chose pre-med, which led to the real issue.

Tim grew up with a depressed father who treated him harshly and verbally abused his mother who, in turn, also suffered from depression .The picture he painted was of a dark family life; I heard themes of him longing for his father's approval and feeling responsible for his mother's happiness. When we got to the heart of the matter, we discovered he had, unconsciously, chosen pre-med to make his father proud and mother happy, not because pre-med was a good fit for him. He was playing the role of hero by making one of the most important decisions of his life to meet his parents' needs and now found himself trapped. It came as a great relief to be given both permission and encouragement to choose for himself, a tremendous weight lifted from his shoulders. Thankfully, Tim was still young enough to orient himself to his own thinking before he made any more big decisions for the wrong reasons.

If you want to be the adult in the room, you must be able to identify and validate your own thinking. As you process your day-to-day life experience, ask yourself often, "What do I think?" Developing your own thinking requires reserving time for self-reflection. Write down what you have decided are your most important values, beliefs, and life principles. Take time to write your own personal philosophy. Write your own personal vision and mission statement that are truly aligned with who you are, rather than what pleases others. Apply journaling for the purpose of practicing self-reflection. Know in doing these exercises, if your thinking is truly coming from you, it is as valid as what anyone else thinks. As you practice identifying and validating your own thinking, you will experience an empowering sense of growth toward being the adult in the room.

Using the scale from the "Ten Traits of the Adult," circle your level of maturity related to the trait of independent thinking. Then identify a growth goal and one or more specific steps you will begin to take.

You are unable to validate your own thoughts and feelings, and you take most of your cues from others.

You believe in the validity of your own thoughts and feelings and are guided by your own trusted thinking.

1……...…….2……………...3……………...4…………..….5

Growth goal:

Specific steps:

TRAIT THREE

Personal Responsibility

*"Life is what you make it.
always has been, always will be."*

~Grandma Moses

*"We need to get over the questions that focus on the past and on the pain –
'Why did this happen to me?' – and ask instead the question, "Now that this
has happened, what shall I do about it?"*

~ Rabbi Harold Kushner

*"If you don't like something, change it.
If you can't change it, change your attitude.
Don't complain."*

~ Maya Angelou

*"In the long run, we shape our lives, and we shape ourselves.
The process never ends until we die.
And the choices we make are ultimately our own responsibility."*

~ Eleanor Roosevelt

"What? So what? Now what?"

~ Anonymous

Personal Responsibility

*I accept total responsibility for meeting my needs
and for the quality of my life.*

When I begin work with a client, one of the first themes I listen for is personal responsibility. When a client emphasizes her motivation for counseling is to deal with something in her life, I have confidence she will make progress. When a client puts the emphasis on being a victim of circumstance, of the people in her life, and helplessness, I know I have my work cut out for me.

Two people I've worked with, both in their late twenties, who represent opposite ends of the personal responsibility spectrum, come to mind. Amanda was sexually abused over a period of years by her stepfather. Her co-dependent mother refused to believe her and remained in total denial. Amanda was cut off from the outside world and not allowed a social life. When she finally confided in a teacher who attempted to intervene, the family moved out of state where the abuse continued. She lived in a state of fear for years, until in her mid-teens she found the courage to stand up to her stepfather, and the abuse finally ended. I was the first therapist she'd ever spoken to.

What was remarkable was how empowered Amanda was. She was surprisingly mentally and emotionally healthy, given her experiences. Somehow she avoided internalizing a deep sense of shame and victimization. She rejected a belief that her abuse prevented her from succeeding in life. She was in a satisfying marriage and was developing a successful career. Of course, there was still a need to process her abuse in therapy, but her core resilience had sustained her. Her goal in therapy was to increase consciousness of the impact of her experience and to equip herself with the necessary tools to ensure there wouldn't be a barrier to her sustained success and happiness – the essence of personal responsibility. She has been an inspirational example of what people can overcome when they focus on taking responsibility for themselves.

On the other end of the spectrum was Will who had been verbally and emotionally abused by his parents, particularly his mother. When he left home at eighteen, he was completely on his own, without financial or emotional support. He attempted to work his way through college, but dropped out after a couple of years. I initially worked with Will and his wife in marriage counseling, but when it became clear most of their marital problems grew from Will's deeper unresolved anger, I began to work with him individually. We couldn't seem to get past his rage toward his parents. He was stuck in his view that they had ruined his life and sealed his fate. He had a core belief he was a victim and everything wrong in his life was either because of his parents or someone else. Throughout our sessions we spent time processing the impact of his childhood and the validity of his anger, yet he remained unable to shift focus to his responsibility for the quality of his life in the present.

When the adult finds himself in a negative place psychologically or circumstantially, he doesn't waste time or energy placing blame. He holds himself responsible for how he got there and looks to see what he can do to get where he wants to be. He focuses on what is within his control and doesn't dwell on what is outside of his control. The adult view is that he's choosing and creating his life. He can tell you what he wants and envisions for himself. He has a deep understanding of the validity of his needs for safety, love, belonging, respect, empowerment, and purpose. He consciously chooses people and environments that support the meeting of these needs. His self-knowledge helps him gauge what is good and right for him in relationships, marriage, work, and in other areas of life.

The adult can experience being victimized and rendered powerless temporarily, but a state of mind of victimization and helplessness is incompatible with adulthood. The adult has little tolerance for remaining in an unhealthy and damaging environment and will assertively and skillfully articulate feelings and needs and propose constructive solutions. If he has been proactive without progress, he then accepts what is outside his control and makes the best of the situation, or opts to leave peacefully for something healthier.

One of the poorest decisions I've made, many years ago, was taking a job before learning enough about my employer. I immediately realized my mistake when I found the environment unhealthy, stressful, and out of sync with my values. I resigned after just three months without another job lined up – a scary first for me. Nevertheless, I was determined to find a job that met my needs. Thankfully, almost immediately, a right and healthy opportunity presented itself.

Children in grown-up bodies complain often and talk more about what they don't want than what they can envision. They can expound on what hurts, angers them, and what they fear, but when asked what they need, I often hear, "I don't know." Many believe their needs aren't important, or it's selfish to think about their own needs. Many expect others to intuit their feelings and needs. You qualify for adulthood when you know what you want and need and believe those wants and needs are valid. You qualify for adulthood when you can communicate feelings and needs proactively and skillfully.

Ellie was a young woman neglected by her alcoholic father throughout childhood. She was oriented to her fathers' needs and problems at an early age and assumed responsibility for his happiness. Ellie reported a romantic history of bad relationships with men who had also mistreated or neglected her. She interpreted this as just plain bad luck with men. I asked if she dated men who treated her with care and respect. She admitted she didn't stay in relationships with "nice guys" for long because they didn't seem to need her enough, and it felt strange to be treated well. Ellie was controlled by old programs and patterns and felt powerless.

Depending on our experience and our level of self-worth, we develop either a positive or negative comfort zone to take into all areas of our lives. A person with a positive comfort zone expects to have needs met, has little tolerance for being mistreated, and addresses issues assertively. People with negative comfort zones have a high tolerance for not having needs met, live with unhealthy situations indefinitely, and cope with them defensively. Ellie was a classic example of someone who was living life in a negative comfort zone. It takes real commitment to personal growth to re-program a comfort zone, but I regularly witness clients who take responsibility and gain control over meeting their needs.

Abraham Maslow's landmark work during the 1950s and 1960s gave us his hierarchy of human needs, which continues to serve as my most important paradigm for understanding human behavior, motivation, and problems. What Maslow's hierarchy means to me is we humans are instinctively driven to satisfy the same essential needs, starting with physical survival, and progressing to what I think of as second-tier needs which include love, belonging, and self-worth. Once these needs are satisfied, we graduate to the highest level Maslow called self-actualization, which I associate with the need for higher purpose. I equate self-actualization in many ways with mature adulthood.

The theory goes that until we can relax about our basic safety and survival, we can't focus on the next level. For example, we don't worry about self-worth if we're starving. Where we spend most of our mental and emotional energy reveals what needs are most unsatisfied. Most of us are focused on one or more needs in the second tier – love, belonging, and self-worth. Children are dependent on others to meet these needs and spend energy trying to get others to satisfy them. When children don't have needs met, they develop maladaptive behavior patterns in an attempt to feel safe and to gain love, belonging, or self worth.

If you intend to be an adult, you must develop inner resources to meet your own valid needs. In doing so, you take responsibility for the quality of your life. Displayed ahead is a guide to identify the various dimensions within yourself and how to think consciously about taking care of these different parts.

–

Guide to Healthy Self-Care

My Physical Life (My body):

- I view my body as a miracle of creation.
- I trust my body's ability to restore, heal and maintain balance.
- I view my body as a trusted friend and partner.
- I am aware of my body's intelligence.
- I listen to what my body tells me.
- I avoid over-identifying with my body.
- I understand and tend to my body's needs

    Affirmation: I take care of my body by . . .

My Mental Life (My thoughts, beliefs, perceptions, expectations and images):

- I understand how powerfully my thinking influences my experience of life.
- I am aware much of my thinking has formed through a kind of programming process.
- I exercise my power to consciously choose thoughts, beliefs, perceptions, expectations, and images that create feelings of peace, acceptance, trust, love and joy.

    Affirmation: I am increasing my level of peace and happiness by practicing the following beliefs. . .

    I am: _____

    I am: _____

    I am:_____

    Most people: _____

Most people: _____

Most people: _____

Life is: _____

Life is: _____

Life is: _____

My Emotional Life (My feelings):

- I understand the importance of being connected to my feelings.
- I accept responsibility for identifying and resolving my negative feelings.
- I allow myself to experience my feelings without denial or judgment
- I listen to what my feelings tell me.
- I accept responsibility for expressing my feelings constructively.

    Affirmation: I process and manage my feelings by. . .

My Social Life (My relationships):

- I value my needs and others' needs equally
- I practice beliefs and expectations that help me feel connected, trusting, and accepting toward others.
- I am able to initiate contact with others and risk rejection since others can't determine my worth.
- I accept responsibility for getting my needs met in relationships by communicating skillfully.
- I offer others support while allowing the freedom for others to be who they are and to be responsible for themselves.

- I balance listening and talking while interacting with others.
- I move toward healthy people and situations and can peacefully leave unhealthy relationships.
- I establish and maintain healthy boundaries in my relationships.
- I find the balance between time alone with myself and contact with others.

Affirmation: I take good care of myself in my relationships by . . .

My Vocational Life (My work):

- I am discovering my life's purpose and direction.
- I am discovering and expressing my uniqueness – my particular gifts and talents.
- I choose the kind of work and workplace that fits my values and allows me to express who I am
- I am open to change and committed to on-going learning of new knowledge and skill related to my work.
- I take responsibility for getting my needs met in the workplace.
- I focus on being part of the solution to workplace problems and avoid becoming part of the problem.
- I can peacefully leave unhealthy work environments that hold little potential for meeting valid needs.
- I maintain balance in my life by limiting the amount of time I spend focused on work.

Affirmation: I am taking care of myself in relation to my work by . . .

My Recreational Life (My play):

- I cultivate specific non-work activities, hobbies and interests that help me relax, laugh and have fun.
- I accept responsibility for meeting my needs for play.
- I make play time a priority
- I am playful with others.
- I am willing and able to try new activities and learn new skills to meet my play needs.

    Affirmation: I meet my need for play by . . .

My Spiritual Life (My spirit):

- I am connected to a Higher Power.
- I am aware of the spiritual nature in myself and others.
- I am connected to the human family and to the natural world.
- I see the inherent worth in myself and others.
- I consciously practice seeing the miracle, mystery and abundance of life
- I trust life's developmental processes.
- I am learning to be fully present in the here and now of the journey and to lessen my focus on the destination.
- I decide for myself what God means to me by trusting my own thinking, feeling, and experience.
- I take time to listen to God.

    Affirmation: I meet my spiritual needs by . . .

Using the scale from the "Ten Traits of the Adult," circle your level of maturity related to the trait of personal responsibility. Then identify a growth goal and one or more specific steps you will begin to take.

You depend on others to intuit and meet your needs, and you blame others for your unhappiness.

You accept total responsibility for your need satisfaction and the quality of your life.

1............2..............3..............4...........5

Growth goal:

Specific steps:

TRAIT FOUR

Conscious Feeling

"He who angers you conquers you."

~ Elizabeth Kenny

"Let fear be a counselor and not a jailer."

~ Anthony Robbins

"Joy shared is twice the joy. Sorrow shared is half the sorrow."

~ Swedish proverb

"To everything there is a season:
A time to weep and a time to laugh.
A time to mourn and a time to dance."

~ Ecclesiastes

"You are healed of a suffering only by experiencing it to the full."

~ Marcel Proust

"You cannot prevent the birds of sadness from passing over your head, but you can prevent them from nesting in your hair."

~ Swedish proverb

Conscious Feeling

I process and manage my feelings consciously.

As David approached his fiftieth birthday, he took stock of his life for the first time – long overdue. He's a good example of what I call a highly functioning child in a grown-up body. A very successful businessman, David was hard-driving, competitive, entrepreneurial, highly intelligent and fiercely independent. However, he was prone to episodes of explosive anger. And he was an equal opportunity rager. No matter who you were – wife, daughter, friend, colleague, or employee – no one was immune to his outbursts. As a result, his second marriage was hanging by a thread, his relationship with his daughter was strained, he had no close friends, and he had high blood pressure. It was dawning on him that life is short and he was paying a high price for his anger.

Helping someone with anger problems can be a challenge. David was no exception. Not only was his temperament a liability, he had deeper issues. He never knew his father and spent several years of his childhood in boarding schools. He was highly mistrustful of others and had problems with attachment and closeness. I have watched too many good people destroy what's most important to them because they couldn't manage their feelings.

Think of feelings as various types of physical energy that become activated within our bodies. These energies manifest themselves, either positively or negatively, due to a complex bio-chemical reaction triggered by the impact of our day to day life experiences.

The crucial distinction here between the child and the adult is what happens when these energies are negative. Usually we don't have to manage positive feelings like excitement, peace, joy, and love. We just enjoy them. Negative feelings pose challenges. We don't expect a child to have tools to manage negative feelings. When a hungry, tired, child gets frustrated and has a meltdown, hopefully, we can be patient and nurturing while the energy runs its course.

Grown-ups are a different matter. I have been witness to some stunning versions of grown-up temper tantrums in which the energy is in full control. On rare occasions, usually in a marriage counseling session, I've seen grown-ups so overtaken by the negative energy they stood up, flailed, stomped, jumped up and down, screamed, and stormed out of the office. When it's that extreme, whatever is happening in the present is usually triggering a repressed, primal feeling from the past.

People who process and deal with their feelings consciously tend to manage their lives well. People who are controlled by their feelings tend to live stressful lives. The adult has developed conscious insights and coping skills, whereas the child in the grown-up body has few tools.

Clients at times report having had a distressing week or feelings of depression without explanation. It's my job to help them figure it out. "I've had a terrible week. I've felt depressed and I don't know why." So I say, "Then, let's figure it out." Almost always, by the end of the session, we've identified the specific feelings. We've connected the dots as to what triggered the distress. I've been able to teach the key insight and coping skills to be practiced. It's not rocket science, but it does require consciousness.

Insights to practice about feelings:

- **The most powerful energies are attached to our most vulnerable feelings**. Therefore, we must know how to identify them, give them accurate language, connect to them, and allow them to be felt. I observe many people don't have an adequate vocabulary for expressing feelings. They can tell me they are stressed, depressed or angry, which is not very useful. Anxiety and depression are typically symptoms, and anger is usually a defense. Vulnerable feelings are hurt, afraid, lonely, sad, hopeless, ashamed, worthless, and guilty, to name a few. When people are able to identify and own these feelings and accept them as a part of the human experience, they are well on their way to resolving them.

- **Most anger falls under one of two categories – defensiveness and non-acceptance.** Defensive anger is masking and guarding feelings of vulnerability such as hurt, fear, or a sense of inadequacy. Defensive anger often undermines relationships because it overpowers others' attempts to address conflict. For example, it is not uncommon, in couple counseling, to hear a wife tell me she's unable to bring up even the slightest complaint with her husband because he immediately reacts defensively. When we get to the heart of it, oftentimes, I find a man who feels incompetent in aspects of intimacy and hears a simple complaint as confirmation he is, indeed, failing as a husband. This deeper insecurity has to be exposed and addressed consciously, or it will continue to be the source of destructive anger. The more one can express vulnerable feelings, the less one needs defenses.

Anger from non-acceptance surfaces in people who have rigid expectations of how life should and shouldn't be. These people also tend to have a strong sense of right and wrong, justice and injustice. They tend to process in terms of black or white. When they encounter the messiness of life and the flawed nature of people, their non-acceptance often leaves them too angry. These people have to consciously learn how to accept life on its terms. They have to learn how to see the shades of gray. They also have to learn to pick their battles consciously and communicate assertively rather than reactively. Anger due to non-acceptance can also signal unresolved grief related to past events left unaddressed.

- **In general, anxiety is symptomatic of fear, and depression is symptomatic of loss and grief.** If you experience some degree of chronic anxiety, begin to identify your deeper fears and address them. If you experience chronic depression, begin to identify what feels lost to you and needs to be grieved consciously.

Here are the types of fears and losses at the heart of most anxiety and depression:

Fear of. . .	Loss of . . .
illness and death	love and respect
failure	identity and self-worth
rejection	safety and security
disapproval	connection and belonging
losing respect	power and control
losing a loved one or friend	meaning and purpose
losing a job	loved one or friend
going broke	health
losing safety and security	lifestyle
being trapped	hope

- **Feelings must be felt.** Once feeling energy is set in motion, it needs to run its course. One of the best things we can do is consciously identify the feeling, allow it to be felt, and recognize it as the human experience. The worst thing we can do is judge the feeling, try to fight and control it, deny and repress it, or self-medicate it. Taking this approach with negative feelings can get us in serious trouble. There is a Buddhist principle that teaches pain is part and parcel of the human condition and in accepting pain and allowing it to be felt, it becomes manageable. When we fight pain, it controls us.

- **Feelings are driven by thoughts.** There is truth in the old adage, "Our perception becomes our reality." Two people can experience the same circumstance, but be affected in very different ways based on their varying interpretations of their situation. Obviously, people who have predominately positive thoughts and beliefs enjoy more positive feelings than those who think and believe more negatively. Faulty and distorted thoughts and beliefs are at the root of most anxiety, depression, and insecurities. The words and actions of others and life's circumstances are not causes but rather catalysts that activate programs within us that generate our feelings.

There are four categories of thought and belief that encompass our most powerful programs: what we think and believe about ourselves, other people, our future, and life in general. We have the power to re-program, if needed, and consciously choose thoughts and beliefs that enhance our emotional well-being. I elaborate on this principle in an upcoming section.

- **Talking out negative feelings is therapeutic.** There is no virtue in stoicism if you have stored up negative feelings. Let's destroy the myth that it's a weakness to admit vulnerable feelings. Instead, it's an act of maturity to admit you're hurt, afraid, or feel alone, for example. When we secretly hold these energies inside and dwell on them, we begin to lose perspective, our thoughts become increasingly distorted, and the negative energy intensifies. It's as if these feelings take on a life of their own that can seem overwhelming. Something powerful happens when we're able to find the accurate words to describe these feelings and express them to a trusted person who can be supportive. In expressing them, we are no longer alone with them. They are brought down to size and made manageable again.

- **Our bodies sometimes are telling us what we need to know about our feelings.** I mentioned in the preface my minor life crisis in my mid-thirties. I needed to make a career change and provide for my family at the same time. I felt trapped where I was and overwhelmed, knowing what it would take to change everything. I'd suppressed most of these feelings, but my body was telling me loud and clear I couldn't ignore them. I developed classic symptoms of clinical anxiety. I experienced states of fear, which caused my body to overproduce adrenalin. Too much adrenalin causes chronic muscle tension which compresses the spine, pinches the nerves, and short circuits other systems. I had chronic neck and back pain and gastro-intestinal problems which made it difficult to eat. I couldn't sleep, had no energy, couldn't concentrate, and caught colds frequently. When I started having panic attacks, I knew my body was telling me I had to address the real issue instead of all the symptoms. So, I began the process of changing careers, and it was challenging, but the changes made all the difference. I don't like to imagine how I would be doing physically, mentally, and emotionally today, had I ignored what my body was telling me.

- **Crying is a good thing**. Crying is a healthy mechanism for releasing strong, pent-up, emotional energy. Yes, men need to cry. Suppressing a needed cry is not healthy. The next time you feel the impulse to cry and you're in a situation that allows for it, make a conscious choice to let it out.

- **Because of the indelible link between body, mind, and emotions, taking good care of your body needs to be an essential strategy for enhancing your emotions.**

Healthy eating and regular exercise help create the chemicals for a sense of emotional well-being. Don't expect to feel good emotionally with a lifestyle of poor eating and no exercise.

- **Because many of our negative feelings stem from our interaction and needs related to other people, assertiveness skills are required for managing feelings.** The child in the grown-up body is unable to make himself effectively understood; whereas, the adult has developed the assertiveness skills necessary for getting his needs met. I elaborate on this point further in the upcoming section on assertiveness.

- **Sometimes unresolved, repressed feelings get triggered.** Imagine the man who, as a child, was verbally abused by his father and now works for a boss who has similar traits as his father. On days he experiences the slightest tension with his boss, he sinks into a dark mood for the rest of the day. The mood is out of proportion to the situation, but he doesn't know what his own mood is really about. He experiences this from time to time, and it seems inexplicable to him, but it's clearly not a mystery. A child in a grown-up body can be held hostage by these repressed, unresolved feelings. The adult who has experienced this has addressed this pattern proactively and has connected the dots. He has identified the deeper wounds of hurt, fear, shame, and anger he feels in relation to his father. He has learned to recognize the triggers such as an encounter with an authority figure similar to his father. He has learned, on the one hand, how to allow himself to feel old feelings and, on the other hand, to reassure himself his boss is not his father and he's not a helpless, little boy.

- **Dwelling on negative feelings intensifies them.**
  Imagine two people who come to therapy reporting
  symptoms of depression. One person tells me that
  between her work and her children she doesn't have time
  to dwell on how she feels. The other person tells me she
  has a lot of idle time and winds up dwelling on her
  feelings. Guess who improves faster? Obviously, the one
  who has other constructive things to focus on. If you are
  dealing with negative feelings, along with applying the
  other insights and skills I've emphasized, make sure you
  stay active and focused on other matters enough to avoid
  dwelling on how you feel.

Angie, who was in her mid-forties, came to counseling seriously
depressed. A classic example of what can happen when you lack
the tools to process and manage feelings consciously, Angie came
out swinging, so to speak, when she was betrayed by her best
friend and her boyfriend, whom she discovered had been sexually
involved. This betrayal had so much power over her that her
vindictive reactions did more damage to her than the betrayal.
Many of the friends she and her best friend shared lost respect for
her because of the destructive way she tried to involve them.
Angie knew her anger was eating her, but she didn't know how to
escape it other than to drink too much. To top it off, a good
friend was telling her the right thing to do was to forgive them
and move forward, as if she could flip a switch. This caused her to
condemn herself for her anger, which only added to the distress.

Here is what we had to process consciously to help her: First, I
gave her permission to have all of her feelings, particularly her
anger. I underscored she shouldn't be expected to quickly forgive
and move on. Forgiveness, or what I prefer to call acceptance, is
the end stage of a complicated grief process that in Angie's case
would take time. Angie was so stuck in her anger, she'd yet to
make real contact with her more vulnerable feelings – her deep

hurt, rejection, sense of inadequacy, and loss. I ushered her to these powerful emotions to help her feel them and grieve. I helped her recognize her self-worth was too defined by the men in her life and by outside approval, which gave this betrayal disproportionate power. We began to focus on strengthening her sense of self. Unfortunately, this entire episode came when she was temporarily unemployed with all her time dedicated to obsessing over the sordid details. Angie's thoughts dwelled on how she'd been victimized, so we strategized to create more productive activities for herself in order to shift her focus and feel empowered. As a result of processing her experience consciously with these new tools, her anger and depression began to lift and she was able to begin moving forward.

As you can see, there is much to understand about how feelings work and how to manage them. Feelings in a child mostly function unconsciously and overpower the child at times. Adults have learned how to identify their feelings consciously and manage them.

Here are some questions to ask the next time you feel some significant distress.

What am I feeling, especially on a vulnerable level?

What is this feeling really about for me?

Is it the fear of something or the loss of something?

Is it about an unmet need?

Is it about a deeper insecurity within me?

Is it just about the present, or is it related to past unresolved feelings?

What has happened that has triggered this feeling?

How can I address it proactively?

Do I need to talk this out with someone?

Do I need to be more assertive, recruit understanding, and ask for what I need?

Do I need to work on accepting something that is hard to accept?

Do I need to change the way I think?

Do I need to find constructive things to focus on to avoid dwelling on how I feel?

Using the scale from the "Ten Traits of the Adult," circle your level of maturity related to the trait of conscious feeling. Then identify a growth goal and one or more specific steps you will begin to take.

| You are often controlled by your feelings. | You often process and manage your feelings consciously. |

1…….…...2…………...3…………...4…….…...…5

Growth goal:

Specific steps:

TRAIT FIVE

Positive Core Beliefs

"As a man thinketh in his heart, so is he."

~ Proverbs

"If you believe you can, you probably can.
If you believe you won't, you most assuredly won't."

~ Denis Waitley

"We are shaped by our thoughts.
We become what we think."

~ Buddha

"The mind is its own place, and in itself, we can make a heaven of hell, and a
hell of heaven."

~John Milton

"You find what you look for – good or evil, problems or solutions."

~ John Templeton

Positive Core Beliefs

*I consciously choose thoughts and beliefs
that enhance the quality of my life.*

John arrived at work in a good mood, feeling all was well. He entered his workplace with a smile on his face as he started his walk down the hallway toward his office. The walk took him past several co-workers' offices and as he passed one of the offices, he inadvertently overheard his name mentioned by one co-worker talking to another, though he didn't hear anything else. As he continued walking, his mood began to shift. As he settled in at his desk, he felt distracted and slightly discordant. As the morning progressed, his mood continued to go downhill and by lunchtime he was mildly depressed. It was a mystery to John as to why his mood shifted so dramatically so quickly. He complained of having these inexplicable changes in mood on a regular basis – a phenomenon millions of people experience daily. Many people are acutely aware of how they feel, but totally unaware of the thought process that leads to their feelings. The unconscious thoughts triggered by something as inadvertent as hearing his name mentioned held the keys to John's moods. Overhearing someone mention our name can automatically activate an inner dialogue that reflects what we believe about ourselves. John was unconsciously imagining his co-workers deriding him, a thought process which flipped the "on" switch to a whole computer program in him listing all the defects that confirm his core belief that something is wrong with him. As he obsesses on these distorted thoughts, his mood darkens.

From the earliest stages of our development through our childhood and adolescence, we form foundational, patternized ways of thinking and perceiving. Our experience of life bombards us with information and messages, both verbal and non-verbal, that we begin to interpret. Quite naturally, at early ages we get most of our information from parents and family members, teachers, and peers. The way we interpret all of this information forms the basis for our core beliefs. Once core beliefs form, they become, perhaps, the most powerful force in our lives. While we grow up and experience life, we internalize beliefs about ourselves, others, life in general, and our future.

These beliefs become the filters through which we process and interpret our experiences. Two people can experience the same event, but be affected in opposite ways because of their difference in perception based on different core beliefs. Obviously, the kind of environment in which we grow up, the extent to which we get our needs met, and the quality of our learning are powerful influences on our core beliefs. Those who were fortunate enough to internalize positive core beliefs are equipped to have a relatively smooth transition to adulthood. Many people have to overhaul their core beliefs to make the transition, and some people never resolve these barriers to adulthood.

For many of us, core beliefs are so deeply embedded they function unconsciously. Negative, unconscious core beliefs lead to negative, unconscious thoughts and feelings that result in negative, unconscious behavior. This dynamic inhibits maturational growth. I'm so attuned to this frequency, it doesn't take me long with a client to hear what they cannot. They may not use the exact words, but the belief comes through loud and clear. These are some of the most common themes I hear:

> I'm not good enough
> Something is wrong with me.
> I don't belong.

You can't trust people.

Bad things are going to happen. I can't handle it.

Life is too hard.

I'm responsible for everything

I have to please everybody.

I have to be perfect.

I'm helpless.

The world is a dangerous place.

I will fail.

I will be rejected.

Laura was a thirty-five year-old woman who entered counseling reporting she'd struggled with depression off and on as long as she could remember. As we explored, she spoke of how alone and isolated she felt and how she longed for more friendships and social connections. She explained that when she attempted to participate in social groups, she felt unwelcomed, left out, and subtly rejected. She said this seemed to happen to her consistently. I then began to tune in on the core belief frequency because it didn't add up otherwise. I was already struck by her likeable personality and her delightful sense of humor.

Laura explained that when she entered a group, her perception was everybody there "had it made." They all knew each other, they were all comfortable and belonged, and they seemed to ignore her and leave her out. At times, she assumed people were judging her. Eventually, she found herself on the periphery, feeling awkward and hurt. She also assumed there must be something wrong with her.

I asked Laura to try to remember when she first experienced this in her life. After a few moments of reflection, she remembered she first experienced rejection when she was eleven years old. She explained she grew a foot taller that year. She grew so tall, so fast, she towered over all her classmates, including the boys. For several years she was teased and ridiculed mercilessly by other kids.

So there it was: real rejection at a very vulnerable age that had an indelibly painful impact and planted the seeds of "I don't belong" and "Something's wrong with me." At thirty-five Laura was still processing parts of her life with the mind's eye of that deeply insecure eleven-year-old girl. I could see that she was connecting the dots for the first time in her life.

I explained that we all develop programs comprised of core beliefs and when we have childhood experiences like hers, we're at risk when we're children to internalize distorted beliefs about ourselves and our world. Then, we typically spend the rest of our lives twisting and turning perceptions in order to confirm those beliefs; and we always find what we're looking for, sometimes ignoring obvious contradictory evidence.

Laura was a pleasure to work with because she was open to seeing how this was affecting her life and was ready to re-program. I asked her to practice observing her own self-talk and her predisposition to look for evidence of rejection by reading people's minds and their body language, assuming the worst, all of which was controlling her unconsciously.

When Laura attended future gatherings, she practiced thinking everyone in the room was in the same boat, all with flaws, insecurities, and issues to deal with; they were busy worrying about themselves and had no reason to judge her. I asked her to consider that others were probably new to the group too and trying to find their place. I also asked her to practice telling herself she did belong as a member of the human family. As she practiced this new awareness and cognitive skill, her experience improved fairly quickly. She reported that as she practiced this view, she relaxed. As she relaxed, her natural likeability came out and others responded. She could tell she was more approachable, and she was able to take a few more risks. She could see, indeed, there were others new to the group. She began to reach out to them and they responded. By the time we ended our work together, Laura was functioning at a new level of consciousness that was dramatically improving the quality of her life.

I've observed so many different version of this dynamic in people's lives:

- There was the woman whose father openly and repeatedly cheated on her mother. She internalized "You can't trust men," and was constantly suspicious and accusatory of her husband while there was abundant evidence of his love and commitment.

- There was the man who, as the oldest child in a family with an extremely abusive father, assumed the caretaker role in his early teens by trying to protect his mother and his siblings from his father. He'd spent his life believing he was responsible for the happiness of everyone close to him. He was burning himself out, trying to rescue and protect them and to fix everything for them.

- There was the woman who was the lost child in her chaotic family. She internalized she wasn't important to anyone and would constantly look for the evidence to confirm her insignificance to her husband, children, and co-workers, when in reality she was highly valued by them.

This diagram is a way of visualizing how core beliefs can work in our lives.

Negative Version

Core belief: "Something is wrong with me."

↓

Trigger: A friend gives me an odd look that confuses me.

↓

Interpretation: "He must be mad at me for some reason. I don't
(self-talk)   know what I did wrong. This always happens

when I make a friend. Once they get to know me, they dump me; I'm such a loser."

↓

Feelings: Confusion, hurt, fear, loneliness, shame

↓

Behavior: Withdrawal or defensiveness

Positive Version

Core belief: "I am acceptable as I am."

↓

Trigger: A friend gives me an odd look that confuses me.

↓

Interpretation: "I don't know what that look meant. He could be
(self-talk)   having a bad day. I know I haven't done anything
                 intentionally to offend him, so it probably has
                 nothing to do with me. If he's displeased with me
                 for some reason, I'll let him be responsible for
                 letting me know. If it continues, I will ask him if
                 something is going on."

↓

Feelings: Minor, temporary confusion

↓

Behavior: Unaffected

Craig entered counseling because he'd been bitterly unhappy in his marriage for years. He explained he knew the marriage had been a mistake almost from the beginning and it only got progressively worse. He described a hellish picture that seemed to merit a divorce, but, as much as he wanted out, he couldn't bring himself to leave. After a little exploring, the answer to his immobility became clear. I asked Craig to describe what he envisioned beyond a divorce. He had never identified this consciously before, but the picture that emerged was stunning. He told me he imagined growing old alone and isolated. He expected his friends and colleagues would judge him. He anticipated feeling like a failure and carrying powerful shame and guilt. What was most insidious was his belief God might punish him by causing him to lose his job – the thing he loved and valued the most. To top off this list of distorted beliefs, he saw himself as powerless to create something better. Craig's picture of life beyond divorce was worse than life in his marriage. Why would anyone choose to go from bad to worse? I explained unless he believed he was capable of creating a better life for himself and could envision a more positive future, he would not have the motivation to leave. It was a revelation to him to bring to consciousness his own dark and distorted thoughts, beliefs, and images that kept him trapped. I find this explains why many people remain in unhealthy and destructive environments.

We all have to learn to practice thinking consciously to be in control of our lives and be the adult in the room. It is a challenge for all of us. For example, those of us who are self-employed can sometimes feel insecure. There are occasions when my practice slows and I see holes in my schedule. My first impulse is to doubt myself and question my competence. I can feel the panic as I picture going out of business and subsequently going broke. I catch myself, first own my fear, then remind myself of the positive feedback I receive and the times I've had a waiting list. I remind myself of the ebb and flow of any business. Finally, I affirm that if my worst fears were realized, I would figure out a way to deal with them.

Adults have developed the consciousness that enables them to intentionally cultivate positive core beliefs. They're able to monitor their thoughts in order to identify and to correct the distorted ones and to choose healthy ones. They catch it when they're beating themselves up, trying to read someone's mind, or twisting a perception to confirm a negative belief. Then they choose empowering thoughts and beliefs.

Examples of Empowering Self-Talk:

> I am acceptable as I am.
> I'm a work in progress.
> I can be flawed and imperfect and make mistakes.
> We are all in the same boat; everybody has their own issues.
> We are all connected as human beings.
> I can take responsibility and learn and grow.
> I can learn to deal with whatever I have to face.
> I can ask for help.
> I have valid thoughts, feelings, and needs.
> I have the power to get my needs met and make myself happy.
> Most people have good intentions.
> Most people are doing the best they know how.
> I'm not responsible for other people's happiness.
> I can take the risk; I'll still be OK.
> I expect good things to happen.
> I am capable.

When I'm helping someone learn to think more consciously, I sometimes give a practice assignment using the universal circumstance of being stuck in traffic. I first ask them to practice observing their feelings and their self-talk while they are driving in traffic. Of course, most report feeling something on the continuum between mild frustration and intense rage. I'm not concerned about mild frustration, which is inevitable, but anger and rage are clearly problematic as well as dangerous. Not surprisingly, people who experience anger or rage are thinking incredibly distorted thoughts, most of which have been unconscious and automatic.

Examples of Distorted Thoughts While Driving in Traffic:

> I shouldn't have to put up with this.
> My taxes are being wasted.
> This is the worst time for this construction.
> The people in the highway department are all idiots.
> Nobody knows how to drive; they're all idiots.
> He's not getting away with cutting me off; I'll show him.
> This better not make me late.
> Being late is going to make me look bad.
> I should have left earlier; I'm an idiot.
> I have no control over my life.

The next step is re-scripting. Sometimes I actually write out some coping statements for clients to take and practice in the particular situation we are targeting.

Coping Self-Talk for Traffic:

> This is a reality of life; I can accept it.
> The construction will eventually make this better.
> Everybody around me is going through this; we're all in the same boat.
> If other people can deal with this, I surely can.
> Most everybody is doing the best they can under the circumstances.
> I'm not going to let someone else's recklessness have the power to disturb me.
> I have to let go of what is out of my control.
> Most people have experienced this and will understand if I'm late.
> This is a learning experience; I will be prepared next time.
> I can control how I think about this.

Apply this practice to something in your life that causes you distress on a regular basis. Maybe it's a situation at work with a co-worker or a boss. Maybe it's a particular circumstance that is out of your control. Perhaps there is something stressful you're anticipating. Maybe you're having to cope with a situation involving a friend or a family member.

Once you have identified the situation, begin to observe consciously how you're thinking about it and particularly your self-talk. Next, evaluate how your thoughts are making you feel and whether or not that's what you want. Then determine if a different way of thinking about the situation would help you cope better. This may seem like common sense, but all of us have blind spots that need more consciousness.

If you want to know more about your own core beliefs, pick up the book *Prisoners of Belief* by Matthew McKay and Patrick Fanning. Theirs' is the best core belief assessment tool of which I am aware. David Burns' bestseller, *The Feeling Good Book* also does an excellent job of explaining how distorted thought patterns are the root cause of many people's anxiety and depression. Susan Jeffers' book *Feel the Fear and Do It Anyway* is another excellent resource for this topic. Anything Wayne Dyer has written or recorded will be very helpful and instructive related to higher consciousness and the power of thoughts and beliefs.

Finally, take a few minutes to reflect on your life going back to your childhood. Review your experience in your family with parents and siblings. Review your experience in school and with teachers and peers. Assess these experiences.

- How well were your needs met?

- What messages do you think you received about yourself, your life, your future, and other people?

- Were there particular experiences that stand out to you that strongly affected you positively or negatively?

- What beliefs did you internalize along the way about yourself, your life, your future, and other people?

Using the scale from the "Ten Traits of the Adult," circle your level of maturity related to the trait of positive core beliefs. Then identify a growth goal and one or more specific steps you will begin to take.

You are often controlled
by unconscious, negative
thoughts and beliefs.

You often consciously
choose thoughts and
beliefs that enhance the
quality of your life.

1………..……..2……………...3……………...4…………..….5

Growth goal:

Specific steps:

TRAIT SIX

Insight

"Things are seldom what they seem."

~ Sir William Gilbert

"We don't see things as they are; we see them as we are."

~ Anais Nin

"Beware lest you lose the substance by grasping at the shadow."

~ Aesop

"You can never solve a problem on the same level as the problem."

~ Emmet Fox

"You fear what you do not understand."

~Anonymous

Insight

I am developing key insights that equip me to understand the complexities in life and to respond effectively.

We've all heard, "Don't take it personally." But why are some people better than others at knowing what to take to heart and what to take in stride? There are several keys to this answer, but our level of insight is a major factor.

It's instinctual to feel threatened by, or to judge, what we don't understand. Insight is the knowledge necessary to understand why something or someone behaves in a certain way. Understanding, in most cases, lessens our sense of threat and defensive responses. With understanding, our responses tend towards the positive, strategic, and effective. For example, what, in ancient times, was thought to be demon possession, we now understand as mental illness, thanks to our greater knowledge of brain function and chemistry. This understanding enables us to respond with compassion rather than judgment and fear. Likewise, because of our knowledge of weather patterns, we understand why certain natural disasters occur and can plan for them. We no longer view them as random expressions of God's wrath.

Remember the old adage, "If your only tool is a hammer, then every problem is a nail?" Insights are tools; the more you have, the more equipped you are to respond effectively to the challenges you face every day.

Consider these common scenarios:

- A couple lacking insight about personality traits with frequent communication problems: she processes emotionally; he processes analytically. When she tries to talk about what distresses her at work, she perceives his response to be cold and uncaring. He thinks he is helping by pointing out what she is doing wrong and giving advice to solve the problem. She begins to avoid sharing personal feelings and harbors resentment.

- A father who lacks insight about a child's needs and responds with only frustration and irritation to his child's attention-seeking behavior

- A boss lacking human motivation insight who uses fear and intimidation to increase the productivity of employees

- The well intentioned mother lacking insight about child development who overprotects her children and does everything for them

- The husband whose wife feels unloved when he works long hours, while he views providing for her as the ultimate expression of his love

- A manager who doesn't understand the power of modeling and exhibits behavior that contradicts her expectations of staff

- The father who lacks insight about attention-deficit disorder and perceives his son's distractibility, impulsivity, and pattern of not completing tasks as laziness or defiance

- The couple who has little understanding of conflict resolution and allows their defenses to control their interactions

- The extraverted husband who perceives his introverted wife is shutting him out when she withdraws into a book after a long, stressful day

The adult has accumulated a toolbox full of insights. And though we learn many of our insights through the natural process of life lessons, the learning doesn't happen by osmosis. Gaining insight requires the intention to learn what life can teach us. I work with people regularly who have repeated negative patterns over and over with the same negative results and still can't tell me what they have learned from their experiences. The adult learns from life lessons with the conscious intention to make course corrections along the way.

The adult has learned the human experience is complex and there are rarely simple explanations and quick solutions to problems. Even life lessons are not enough to equip the adult for all challenges.

Adults have come to realize that each area of life – relationships, marriage, parenting, and work – require unique insights to master. They invest energy in learning what is required to increase effectiveness and happiness in these parts of life through formal means such as reading, seminars, classes, counseling, contemplation and reflection, and astute observation of positive models.

One of the most empowering and far-reaching insights I've gained through my work is that **most human behavior makes perfect sense**. Therefore, when I encounter behavior – particularly negative behavior I don't understand, don't relate to, or even find abhorrent – rather than judge it, I'm inclined to try to make sense of it. Alternatively, when we judge what we don't understand, we're more likely to react defensively and ineffectively. When I seek to find an explanation for negative behavior, my mind stays open; I do more listening and respond strategically, not reactively. I know that when I judge behavior and defend against it, I actually empower it. And likewise, when I'm open to understanding, I'm better positioned to influence it.

Human behavior is largely a reflection of the following aspects of our lives: our level of need satisfaction, our learning, our personalities, and our emotions. The following insights are essential tools for practicing a mature level of consciousness.

Our needs: Human behavior is motivated by fundamental needs.

In general, people whose needs are satisfied have positive behavior patterns. People who have unsatisfied needs develop negative, maladaptive behavior patterns in their attempt to satisfy needs. When I encounter negative behavior, one of my first questions is, "What need is this behavior attempting to meet?"

An example of this insight comes from an early experience, while in college, when I served as a part-time houseparent for foster children. One particular teenager in the group was notorious for taking food from the kitchen and hiding it in his room. On the surface, it appeared he was a thief. When I learned his history, however, I discovered that throughout his childhood he had to worry about whether he would have enough to eat. What people steal can tell us what their unmet needs are. If someone steals something of status, for example, the behavior is usually an attempt to meet a self-worth need.

The phenomenon of gang behavior is an extreme, but valid, illustration of the connection between behavior and needs. As reprehensible as gangs may seem, their existence makes perfect sense. In communities where gangs thrive, they are often perceived by the members as being the only resource for safety, belonging, self-worth, and empowerment. These needs are so powerful they can motivate people to commit violent and criminal acts. Communities that successfully deal with gangs have done so by meeting the needs of their youth with a focus on strengthening support systems, rather than solely relying on policing gangs out of existence.

When we have the insight to recognize negative behavior as an attempt to meet a need and not just pass judgment, we can respond on the need level and be effective. The next time you encounter a behavior you don't understand, even your own behavior, ask yourself if this is about an unmet need.

The following are examples of maladaptive behavior patterns related to unmet needs for safety, love, belonging, self-worth, and empowerment:

- Fight or flight behavior patterns
- Risk avoidance
- Manipulation
- Over-control
- Lying, deceiving, denying responsibility
- Stealing
- Passive/aggressive expression of negative feelings
- People-pleasing (gaining approval and avoiding disapproval)
- Care-taking (assuming too much responsibility for others)
- Tolerating mistreatment
- Promiscuity
- Having affairs
- Judgmental thinking and criticism
- Over-achievement and under-achievement
- Emphasis on image
- Perfectionism
- Attention-seeking

Consider this list of maladaptive behaviors and imagine how each might reflect a specific need or two. Assess whether or not you exhibit one of these patterns that might be symptomatic of unmet needs. Identify someone you know who fits one of these patterns and connect it to their probable needs. The more you see people in this light, the more effective you will be interpersonally as a result of your increased level of understanding and compassion.

Our learning: Most human behavior is learned.

In general, people behave the only way they know how, based on their learning. Our family culture is the primary source of early learning. The larger culture surrounding us is also a powerful influence on learning. Another question to ask when encountering negative behavior is, how was this behavior learned?

Ryan and Claire are a good example. Any conflict could trigger Claire to go on the attack, yelling and screaming at Ryan, provoking him to completely withdraw and even leave their home at times. I asked them to step back and recall how their respective families dealt with conflict. Claire stated that in her family they yelled and screamed. Ryan shared that in his family conflict was avoided at all cost. It was a revelation to them to realize they were each unconsciously re-enacting what they learned from their parents. This insight motivated them to learn to deal with conflict constructively. Next time you encounter confusing behavior, consider what it might explain about one's learning.

Examples in life that may reflect early learning:

- Everyday life skills such as personal hygiene, money management, organization
- Communication patterns and level of interpersonal skill
- Reaction to conflict
- Vocabulary
- The role played in relationships
- Approaches to parenting
- How feelings are dealt with
- Awareness and understanding of boundaries
- Decision-making and problem-solving skills
- Self-control and self-discipline
- Work ethic
- Personal responsibility
- Values and beliefs

I've encountered grown-ups who can't take care of their own laundry, usually a hangover from well-intentioned parents who managed all the chores, while others struggle to manage money – either because they were over-indulged growing up or maybe had no expendable money at all. People who routinely use profanity likely experienced it as normal language in their family or culture while growing up. How does a father know how to function in his role if he grew up without a father or with an abusive one? An individual who is insensitive to the privacy and personal space of others likely grew up in an environment where boundaries were routinely violated. People's indecisiveness can reflect their having had too many decisions made for them during childhood. Someone without self-control, in many cases has witnessed out-of-control behavior during formidable years or may have never been disciplined. Someone with a poor work ethic or a low level of personal responsibility may have seen it modeled, or was not expected to assume personal responsibility in early life. Likewise, prejudice and bigotry are values often learned at a young age and in family life.

This insight, that most human behavior is learned, equips us to engage the behavior with more patience and, at times, even the compassion required to have a positive influence on the behavior.

Consider the previous list and apply it to your own learning and behavior. Is there something new you need to learn? Apply this insight to yourself and people you encounter each day.

Our personality: Most human behavior is an expression of personality.

In general, most behavior is a reflection of personality traits – our wiring. I use the *Myer-Briggs Personality Inventory* framework for understanding personality differences. Some people are more extraverted – outgoing, talkative, and social, while others are more introverted – quiet, reserved, and introspective. Some process life emotionally, while others process analytically. Some people tend to be practical, realistic, and detail-oriented, while others lean towards the creative, imaginative, and visionary. People can be organized, decisive, and task-oriented or spontaneous, laidback, and playful. When I don't understand a behavior, I ask myself what personality trait does this behavior reflect?

Lack of insight, regarding personality, is often at the heart of my work with married couples. Here is a classic example: One partner has a need for the physical environment at home to be neat, orderly, and clutter free, while the other is less aware of the physical surroundings and lives comfortably with disorder and clutter. Invariably, a power struggle develops as they judge and try to change each other. One behavior is viewed as lazy and irresponsible, while the other is viewed as controlling and perfectionistic. Their critical evaluations can grow contempt and damage the love and respect they have for each other. My work is to help them understand their differences more objectively and to teach them how they can accept each other. Only then can they learn to negotiate solutions.

Examples of how lack of personality insight can lead to misperceptions and real misunderstanding:

- Highly introverted personalities can be perceived as unapproachable, snobbish, rejecting, even angry or depressed. In reality, an introvert can become so acutely preoccupied in an inner world of thoughts and feelings that his concentration can make him appear intense, serious, and closed-off. When people have to guess what's going on with the introvert, the only thing they may have to go on is silence and a frown. Often introverts are slow to warm up, but once comfortable, can be as warm and funny as anyone. Consider the people in your life you first knew to be shy, but now know very well. Because introverts are introspective, they sometimes offer the world our deepest insights. They can also offer others some of the deepest friendships.

- Highly extraverted personalities can sometimes be perceived as coming on too strong, not listening, rude, gossiping, or shallow. In reality, extraverts are wired to spend energy and to process thoughts and feelings out loud. They are compelled to take initiative and to engage people. They don't tolerate, for very long, being out of touch with people. Because extraverts generate action and connectivity, they can be the life of the party, energize activities, and provide dynamic leadership.

- Highly creative and imaginative personalities can be perceived as absent-minded, flaky, impractical, and even weird. These are people who are compelled to think outside the box. They can become immersed in their imaginations and tune the real world out. They can also live in the world of the theoretical, abstract, and unknown. These personalities can produce our artists, poets, musicians, writers, physicists, and philosophers.

- People who are wired for planning and organizing can be perceived as perfectionists, controlling, inflexible, and too intense. In reality, they have a compelling drive for a sense of completion and closure. They can't help but anticipate what needs to be done, no matter how trivial the task, and cannot rest until it is checked off the list. Completion gives them a sense of control, accomplishment, order, and it lowers their stress. The world would be in chaos without these personalities.

- Highly analytical personalities can be perceived as cold, critical, and uncaring. In reality, their analytical nature is wired to diagnose and solve problems. In a sense, their caring is expressed by trying to fix problems. Analytical thinking is critical thinking that is seeking to find the flaw so it can be corrected. Unfortunately, this way of processing often lacks awareness of the emotional climate and fails, at times, to empathize. These personalities produce our engineers, inventors, scientists, mathematicians, and problem-solvers of all kinds.

- Emotional personalities can be perceived as irrational, over-dramatic, too soft-hearted, and weak-minded. In truth, these personalities process life through the filter of affect. They experience feelings much like they breathe, intuitively. They are intensely aware of others' and their own emotions. This compels them to be emotive as well as to empathize and to nurture. These are the personalities that inspire, generate passion, and make the world a more loving place.

We all have a personality profile that explains much about our behavior patterns. My view of people starts with the premise that we all have a set of strengths and a set of limitations based on our personalities. When I encounter someone reflective of different traits than mine, my insight reminds me of their probable strengths and helps me view them in a positive light to better interact with them.

Our emotions: Human behavior, at times, is an expression of emotional energy.

Often our behavior is a non-verbal way of expressing feelings. It's important to understand that feelings represent physical energy in our bodies created by a variety of chemical reactions in our brain, muscles, organs, and nervous system. There are times when this energy builds to the point of expressing itself behaviorally. Underlying many negative behaviors are feelings of shame, guilt, fear, worthlessness, hurt, anger, and helplessness, just to name a few. A child's temper tantrum is a perfect illustration of how this works. Unfortunately, I too often witness the grown-up versions of temper tantrums. When I encounter negative behavior that seems to be driven by emotional energy, I ask myself what feelings are at the heart of this?

Our sons played basketball when they were teenagers, and I logged many hours in the bleachers rooting for them and, on occasion, yelling at refs. In a particularly close and intense game, our son, Graham, stole the ball and headed towards an unobstructed path to what should have been an easy lay-up on the other end of the court. As he went up for the shot, the player chasing him blatantly shoved him to prevent the basket. Graham went crashing into the wall behind the goal. As soon as I could tell Graham was OK, I called for the ref, from my seat in the stands, to eject the player for such a flagrant and dangerous foul. That's when I heard a distant voice calling me to "shut-up." With confusion, I looked in the direction of the voice and there stood a father of a boy on the opposing team, though not the one who committed the foul. When we made eye contact, he pointed his finger at me and yelled, with fire in his eyes, "That's right. I'm talking to you." I was both dumbfounded and distracted and turned my attention to Graham, who was about to shoot his free throws, though I did manage to say dismissively back, "Well, I'm not talking to you." That was all it took for this father to start marching toward me. At this point I realized this guy was about to lose all control and his anger was not about me. Now only ten feet from me he threatened, "Let's take this outside." Everybody in the stands was watching. I could have ignored him, which probably would have kept him hungry for a reaction. And I could have stood up and defiantly told him to back off, which would certainly have fueled his anger. And I suppose I could have gone outside to experience my first fist fight, but instead, I remained in my seat, turned towards him, and in a calm voice said, "Look man, I have nothing against you, and I'm not going to fight you." He stood there speechless for a few seconds and then stormed out of the gym.

I had the insight to see, early on in this episode, that this was an angry man looking for a fight. I was sad to see this man's anger control his behavior and make him act so childishly. I wondered that day what kind of damage his anger does to him and to his family. I also wondered what had happened in his life that accounted for so much anger. The more I thought about it, the more compassion I felt for him.

I'm glad I had the insight to see he was controlled by his deeper feelings and that I was simply an inadvertent trigger. Insight enabled me to feel calm rather than threatened or defensive, which escalates conflicts. In that moment, insight equipped me to be the adult in the gym.

The world is full of people who carry around repressed emotional energy primed for a spark to ignite tragic outcomes such as destroyed marriages, damaged children, lost jobs, and even jail time. The world is also full of people who, because of circumstances in their private lives, are carrying pain, fear, and grief that cause them to behave in confusing and negative ways. On any given day, these people are in our midst – family members, friends, co-workers, bosses, and strangers with whom we come in contact. This insight into emotions equips us to detect this type of energy early in an encounter and to disarm it by not engaging it defensively. With this insight, we can detach earlier and not take the other's feelings or reactions personally. We are better positioned to help others by allowing them to get the energy out through listening to them and at times getting to what the deeper feelings are really about.

Whether in your work, in a relationship, in marriage, with your children, or with strangers, the next time someone behaves in a way that confuses, offends, hurts, or angers you, first assume there is an underlying explanation. Ask yourself what the behavior might reflect in relation to the other's needs, learning, personality, and emotions. One or more of these usually holds the answer. Insight equips us to relate to others with more peace, acceptance, understanding, forgiveness, and compassion. With insight, you will know better how to respond to others as the adult in the room.

Using the scale from the "Ten Traits of the Adult," circle your level of maturity related to the trait of insight. Then identify a growth goal and one or more specific steps you will begin to take.

You function with little to   You have developed key
no insight and react   insights that equip you to
instinctively to what is on   understand the
the surface.   complexities in life and
                                      respond constructively.

1………..…….2……………....3……………...4………..…….5

Growth goal:

Specific steps:

Assertiveness

"I don't know the key to success, but the key to failure is trying to please everybody."

~ Bill Cosby

"One day Alice came to a fork in the road and saw a Cheshire cat in a tree. 'Which road do I take?' she asked. 'Where do you want to go?' was his response. 'I don't know,' Alice answered. 'Then,' said the cat, 'it doesn't matter.'"

~Lewis Carroll

"By asserting our will, many a closed door will open before us."

~ Seyyed Nasr

"Ask and it will be given to you; seek and you will find; knock and the door will be opened to you"

~ Jesus

Assertiveness

I am asserting thoughts, feelings, and needs skillfully
in order to get my needs met.

If you look closely, you may notice there is an order to my list of adult traits. I have been building the adult from the inside-out. The building blocks of self-acceptance, personal responsibility, conscious thinking and feeling, and insight are the inside traits. We have to build the foundation on the inside in order to practice the skills on the outside. Assertiveness means taking responsibility for expressing skillfully what is on the inside. You have to know who you are and believe in the validity of what you think, feel, want, and need in order to be assertive. Otherwise, when your needs are unmet, you only have instinctive defenses with which to respond.

In my work, I'm often struck by how common it is for grown-ups to deal with issues in their lives passively or aggressively rather than assertively. I'm talking about people who, in many cases, are well-educated and highly accomplished. Many people mistakenly think they're being assertive when they're actually being aggressive. For example, a wife says to me, "He knows exactly how I feel and what I need. I've told him a thousand times!" When I dig into this with her, she eventually admits that her feelings and needs only come out in the heat of arguments when she goes on the attack. I've also observed the reverse of this dynamic when she says, "He knows exactly how I feel because I haven't spoken to him in three days!"

In my view, assertiveness is essential to adulthood. I define assertiveness as the ability to explain to someone, in a rational and respectful tone, what you think and feel, why you think and feel the way you do, what you want or need, and to make a clear and specific request that would help you. Essentially, the goals of assertiveness are to recruit another person's understanding and help in order to satisfy a valid need. Expressing feelings and needs defensively is likely to provoke the other's defenses, inflict more wounds, and create more barriers. We should never expect to get what we want when we are communicating defensively.

Consider this marriage scenario: Tammy has developed resentment toward Kevin and doesn't share her personal feelings about stress at work with him anymore. When she has attempted to do so in the past, he seemed to focus only on what she was doing wrong and what she should do to fix her problems. Occasionally, when Tammy tries to talk with Kevin, the moment he starts to offer advice, she explodes, accusing him of not listening, not caring about her, and of being critical. He then gets defensive. They argue and attack each other until one of them storms out. They cool off and there is no further discussion until the issue is triggered again. In my work with Tammy in therapy, I walked her through these teaching points:

- She is responsible for how she responds, no matter what Kevin has done to trigger her feelings.
- She has to identify the vulnerable feelings below the anger and resentment. What he was doing was causing her to feel hurt, disrespected, and unloved, which was damaging closeness.
- She has to identify what she needs from him. If Kevin listened more for the purpose of understanding and support, she would feel more loved and respected by him and, ultimately, feel closer to him.
- She must first give Kevin's intentions the benefit of the doubt. Her perception of the way Kevin responds might be distorted. His intention may not be as malicious as she thinks. Maybe he is highly analytical and his first instinct is

to focus on diagnosing the problem and what should be done to fix it. Empathy may not come as naturally for him as it does for her.

- She is responsible for organizing these key points into a coherent message and explaining it to him proactively.

- She must request a time to talk when things are calm and emphasize that her intentions are positive. She wants to resolve a barrier in order to feel closer. The timing of the conversation has to be right for both.

- She must preface what she needs to say with statements that help lower his defenses. Use language such as "It seems to me. . ." and "My perception is. . ." Avoid accusatory language such as "You always criticize," or "You never listen."

Here is the essence of the skilled assertiveness Tammy was able to practice with Kevin:

"There is something I want you to try to understand that up to now I have not done a good job of talking with you about. I've allowed resentment to build in me and I'm responsible for that. My resentment is becoming a barrier to feeling close to you, and I want to resolve it so I can feel close again.

Sometimes when I try to talk to you about things that stress or worry me, it seems you focus on what you think I'm doing wrong and what I should change. It feels like you blame me. I don't think you have negative intentions. You may think it helps to give me advice, but I walk away feeling hurt, disrespected, and unloved.

Ultimately, it causes me to feel unsafe in opening up to you. I want you to understand that I need to be able to talk with you about what is going on in my life and feel your support in order to feel close to you. So, the next time I bring these kinds of concerns to you, I would ask that you just listen and try to be understanding without giving me advice or trying to fix it. There are times when I appreciate your advice, but let us agree that if I want it, I will ask for it."

As Tammy continued to practice skillful assertiveness with Kevin, the dynamics in their relationship dramatically improved. Arguments were virtually eliminated. Tammy felt more empowered and less resentful, and Kevin became more sensitive and responsive to her needs.

Another area that requires assertiveness is in our vocational life. As you can imagine, stress caused by job dissatisfaction is a common issue in psychotherapy. Consider Alicia who entered counseling due to symptoms of depression. One of the main issues was her discouragement with work. There were parts of her job she liked and that fit her well, but she was becoming increasingly discontent with the other parts. She could not imagine being in this job for the rest of her life, but didn't know what she really wanted. As we sorted it out, it became clear that the part she really liked was database development. However, her job only allowed her peripheral involvement with database work and she lacked the necessary training and experience to apply for other database jobs.

In order to confirm Alicia's interest, at my recommendation she took *The Highlands Ability Battery*, a natural abilities assessment. Sure enough, her ability profile confirmed her aptitude for database work. Once she identified what she wanted and was able to trust her ability, we focused on how to make it happen. Fortunately, she worked in a large multi-faceted organization where database work was common to several departments. She also had a good track record with the organization and was well-respected, which gave her credibility. It was time for her to start asking for what she wanted.

First, Alicia explained to her department director what she had discovered about herself and the types of new experiences she was now seeking. She submitted a formal, written proposal that was approved, which made it possible for her to fulfill her normal responsibilities while providing her some of the new experience she desired. This, indeed, led to new opportunities that allowed for database training, experience and contact with database staff. Every chance she had, she expressed to the appropriate people what she wanted and her commitment to it. Today Alicia is the manager of a database division at her company. She knows she is now on her right vocational path.

Michael entered therapy struggling with anxiety, depression, high blood pressure, and other stress-related physical problems. It was clear from the first session that he was overwhelmed by demands at work; he felt trapped. As his workload expanded and his anxiety increased, he withdrew socially and even gave up satisfying extracurricular activities. His lifestyle losses added to his depression. Michael was burning out.

He had always been driven; he prided himself on how much he could take on and accomplish and how people could depend on him. He was committed to his work and to his company to a fault. Two years prior to our counseling, he had agreed to add to his already demanding responsibilities the duties of another position after a co-workers' unexpected resignation. His original understanding was that his boss would soon fill the empty position, so his extra workload would be short-lived. Two years later, Michael was still doing the work of two people with no end in sight. It was taking a serious toll on his physical and mental health. I suspected his boss lacked a sense of urgency to hire someone since Michael was doing good work without expressing a complaint.

I asked Michael why he had not been more assertive in discussing the issue with his boss. He explained he was afraid to jeopardize his job; though, as we explored, I heard a more powerful and unconscious barrier. He was so driven by his sense of responsibility that he was out of touch with his own needs and their validity. He believed it was selfish to focus on what he wanted. I had to convince him that to be selfish is to be self-indulgent and that it's healthy, not indulgent, to take good care of himself, to set boundaries and to balance work and personal needs. This was a classic example of someone who could not begin to be assertive until he understood and validated his own needs.

Once Michael was convinced that taking care of his physical and mental health was now a priority, we focused on preparing him to address the issue with his boss assertively. Here is the essence of what he was able to express:

> First, I want you to know I value my job and my association with this organization, and I am very dedicated to its success. I hope to have a long, productive future here.
>
> When Bob left and I took on his territory, I thought there was nothing that I couldn't handle, but over time, I've realized that I have my limits. I've been experiencing some significant stress-related problems for a while now, and I know it's mainly due to feeling overwhelmed managing these two roles. I think I've done a good job covering all of the bases, but my sixty and seventy-hour workweeks have caught up with me.
>
> I have no choice now but to make my health a higher priority. I should have discussed this with you earlier, but I was concerned you might perceive me as less than dedicated. I hope you trust my commitment to our organization.
>
> I'd like to request that we speed the process of my transitioning out of the mid-Atlantic territory so I may focus exclusively on the Southeast. I can respect it if my request is not possible, but I've

concluded that I can't continue in my role as it
stands now. I hope you can respect my dilemma,
and I'm asking for your help.

As it turned out, Michael's boss was totally unaware he was
struggling and responded with sincere concern. Because Michael
was so highly valued, his boss took his request seriously and began
moving on the new hire quickly. Michael returned to his original
sales territory and to a more balanced life. His physical and mental
health gradually improved. He learned an invaluable lesson: to be
in touch with and validate his needs and to assert himself in order
to take care of himself.

Jesus taught, "Ask and it will be given to you; seek and you will
find; knock and the door will be opened to you." This is a
fundamental spiritual principle – know what you want and ask for
it. Consider adding, "do not be easily discouraged," to the adage.
When told "no," press on and keep asking. Offhand, I can't think
of many positive things that have developed in my adult life that I
did not have to ask for.

Another area where assertiveness is crucial is in the lives of those
who exhibit a strong pattern of people-pleasing. This is a
common, but complex, issue in my work with clients. People-
pleasers are usually so oriented to what others think and are in
such need of outside approval that assertiveness is a foreign
language to them. They first have to build a stronger sense of self
by identifying and validating their own thoughts, feelings, and
needs. To help people-pleasers develop assertiveness, I start them
on a basic and incremental level. For example, I ask them to
practice being more conscious of identifying and stating a
preference when asked, rather than deferring to others, with
answers like "it doesn't matter to me," or "Whatever you want."

Examples of assertively identifying preferences:

- I'm in the mood to see a comedy.
- I'd like to try the new Chinese restaurant.

- I would prefer to stay in tonight.
- Let's consider a beach vacation this year.
- I'd like to leave early to avoid the traffic.
- I don't want to spend that much money.
- I'd like to be in by midnight.
- I prefer the darker shade of blue.
- I'd rather adopt a dog than a cat.

Stating a preference is not being selfish. You're not demanding to get your way. You are still sensitive to what the other person wants. You're simply representing yourself in negotiating a decision, which, by the way, most people respect. You should expect, in relationships, a good balance between you and others getting wants satisfied.

People-pleasers find it difficult to say no. Their instinct is to say yes to just about any request, even unhealthy ones. I've observed relationships can feel like traps to people-pleasers because they can't say no. In addressing this pattern with clients, I ask them to practice listening to how they feel when receiving a request. If they spontaneously feel positive and comfortable, then yes is probably the right answer. If there is a feeling of discomfort with the request, then they need to buy some time by asking to be allowed to think about it and respond later. Most requests don't require an immediate response.

With time to think consciously, they can ask themselves a few basic questions:

- What are my needs and priorities right now?
- Does this conflict with my needs and priorities?
- Is this healthy for me?
- Can I say yes, feel right about it, and approach it with the right spirit?
- Is there something I can negotiate in order for me to feel right about this request?
- Is there mutual and balanced sacrifice in this relationship?

Considering these questions will render a conscious and healthy decision as to whether to say yes or no. If the answer is no, people-pleasers have to learn how to say so skillfully. First, we need to understand that if we're dealing with mature people, they will respect our boundaries and our need to take care of ourselves. If we're dealing with immature people, we can't allow their expectations of us to have power. **With that understanding, here are the examples of how to say no:**

- I would like to help you set up your computer tonight, but I've worked some overtime lately and I need to spend time with my kids tonight. I could help you Saturday morning.
- I can go out with you guys tomorrow night, but I'm going to drive separately so I can leave at a decent hour. I haven't been getting enough sleep lately.
- I'm sorry, but I must decline chairing the committee because I have too much on my plate right now, and I don't think I could do it justice.
- I would like to go with you, but I honestly can't afford it right now.
- I hope you understand, but I don't like scary movies. Let me know when you want to see a romantic comedy.

Jessica, a client of mine, wholeheartedly agreed with my assessment that her people-pleasing pattern was controlling her life. During the time we were focusing on this issue with her, she entered into a relationship with a man for whom she was starting to have serious feelings. Jessica observed that historically, for her, the more committed a relationship became, whether it was a friendship or a romance, the more her people-pleasing increased. As she progressed in this new romantic relationship, she was now highly conscious of what to practice to break her old pattern. Her new boyfriend was a "take charge" kind of guy and an avid scuba-driver who was planning a dive trip to Florida and had invited her to join him. She said yes because she wanted to go to Florida with him, but was not interested in scuba-diving. As soon as she said yes, he began to pressure her to take the training class that would certify her to dive with him.

Jessica told me that, in the past, she would have automatically complied with his request and then dreaded the trip because the thought of being hundreds of feet underwater terrified her. Now, however, she was more in touch with her discomfort. With her new consciousness to better listen to and trust herself, this was her response to him:

> When you invited me to join you on your trip, I didn't understand that you expected me to dive with you until you started urging me to take the diving class. I'd like to go to be there with you, but I'm not ready to commit to serious diving. Honestly, the thought of it frightens me. Would you be willing to reserve a little time, while we're there, to take me snorkeling as a first step so I can test out my interest? Otherwise, I'm good at entertaining myself while you dive. If this doesn't work for you, I completely understand. I don't want this to mess up your trip.

Because he was getting serious about her, he, too, wanted her to go with him no matter what and was very understanding and supportive. Not only did her assertiveness result in them having a fun trip, it sensitized him more to her needs.

Assertiveness is the key skill that empowers us to make ourselves understood to the outside world. This skill is required for establishing healthy boundaries in order to take care of ourselves. Assertiveness is a product of a substantial level of growth and maturity and a tangible expression of adulthood. Identify an aspect of your life, either in your relationships or your work, or both, where you can practice more assertiveness.

Using the scale from the "Ten Traits of the Adult," circle your level of maturity related to the trait of assertiveness. Then identify a growth goal and one or more specific steps you will begin to take.

You rely on control,   You assert thoughts and
manipulation, and   feelings skillfully in order
defenses to communicate   to get needs met.
thoughts and feelings to
get needs met.

        1……...……..2……………...3…………….…..4………....…5

Growth goal:

Specific steps:

TRAIT EIGHT

Sacrifice

"The best portion of a good person's life is his little, nameless, unremembered acts of kindness and of love."

~William Wordsworth

"We cannot live only for ourselves. A thousand fibers connect us with our fellow men; and along these fibers, as sympathetic threads, our actions run as causes, and they come back to us as effects."

~Herman Melville

"The joy we feel when we have done a good deed and have lent a helpful hand is the nourishment the soul requires."

~Albert Schweitzer

"One of the deep secrets of life is that all that is really worth doing is what we do for others."

~Lewis Carroll

Sacrifice

*I balance making sacrifices for the needs of others
and tending to my own valid needs.*

Perhaps the most tangible measure of our maturity is our willingness to sublimate our own wants and needs in the service of another or to give ourselves in some way to a purpose that serves a greater good.

One who is quick to do a good deed for someone, does volunteer work, donates money to a worthy cause, or truly listens empathically to people is expressing a compassionate orientation to the needs of others. This ability – to transcend our instinctive drive to put ourselves first – is an adult function. A child in a grown-up body can mimic sacrifice, while the true underlying motivation is mainly self-serving – to gain safety, love, belonging, approval, or self-worth. Many people who did not get important needs met while growing up have real difficulty understanding life outside of their own need-based frame of reference. Their selfishness reflects deep immaturity.

Although today's technology and, in particular, social media have proven they can be used to effect positive life-changing impacts for many people, I see evidence that, for some, their use may be cultivating a self-indulgence and narcissism that can, in effect, create isolation. This downside potential suggests to me that we will be increasingly challenged to avoid getting lost in a virtual world and to stay attuned and connected to real human experience with others. To be truly connected to people involves giving of yourself.

I must confess I've never been a model of sacrifice. What I know about sacrifice I've had to learn as I've matured. I was fortunate to have a comfortable life while growing up, which didn't require much sacrifice on my part. With few exceptions, my first impulse with others had been to focus on what I wanted. Of course, my work oriented me to the needs of others, but it wasn't until I became a husband and later a father that I was fully awakened to life and Catherine teaching me what sacrifice truly meant. I had to develop the consciousness to willingly choose to make sacrifices for my family, and I am still very much a work in progress.

This is exactly my point. The transition from child to adult is not automatic. We have to learn the lesson and then practice the new learning consciously. After years of providing psychotherapy for men and women, I've concluded that, as a rule with plenty of exceptions, the average woman is better equipped for making sacrifices than the average man. The average woman is both wired for and conditioned for nurturing, and, therefore, more oriented to the needs of others and likewise more oriented to sacrifice. The average man is more oriented to freedom, work, and play. As a rule, he has to choose to make sacrifices more consciously, as I have, particularly if he is to be successful as a husband and father.

One of the many small, but symbolic, wake-up calls in my own life occurred on a family vacation at a church retreat in the Ozarks, when our sons were two and five years old. On the morning of our last day I was intently focused on getting our van packed so we could leave on time. I was aware that many of the kids, including my own, and several adults had gathered at the ball field for a send-off softball game, but playing softball was the least of my priorities. I was already stressing about getting home in good time. At some point, Catherine came to the van and appealed to me to come to the field; Graham was getting ready to bat, in a real game, for the first time in his life. I defensively reacted and told her I didn't have the time. After she left, my guilt got the best of me. I reluctantly stopped packing and headed toward the field. I arrived just in time to watch another father patiently showing Graham how to hold and swing the bat and giving him the encouragement he needed while he was batting. I can still recall the lump in my throat and shame I felt as I watched someone else provide Graham with what he needed from his own father.

A lack of sacrifice by husbands and fathers is a common issue in marriage counseling. I work with men who spend too much free time in front of the T.V., on the golf course, or immersed in their computers, playing video games, or other hobbies, while the needs of their wives and children are neglected. To be fair, over my many years of observing marriages and families, I've noted a positive trend in men progressing in their roles and making the necessary sacrifices towards more equitable partnerships.

There is a particular concept known as "maturational loss" that we could all benefit from understanding. The theory goes that with every stage of our lives we will experience certain predictable losses we will have to grieve and eventually accept. During the period of our lives spanning from, roughly, our mid-twenties to our mid-thirties, we adjust to adult responsibilities of full-time work, possible marriage, and parenting. Life becomes more serious when we have to pay the bills. With the new stresses we lose some of the carefreeness, spontaneity, and freedom of childhood. These losses are magnified with the loss of sleep, energy, and money that can accompany life during this phase. There was a period in my early thirties, when our sons were young, I experienced some chronic low-grade depression, accompanied by occasional anger. At the time, I didn't know what was wrong. I only knew I was not my old fun self. In retrospect, it's clear to me that I was grieving classic maturational losses. I wouldn't have been so hard on myself had I understood I was experiencing something so normal.

Through the process of coming to terms with a new reality, one that meant less freedom and play and more responsibility and sacrifice, my internal conflict began to resolve. Gradually, my spirit began to lift. Not only had my resistance to this new reality dissolved, but I also felt a new freedom to give myself more to my marriage and children. I hadn't experienced this type of freedom before. It was deeper and more rewarding than the freedom experienced merely satisfying my own desires and whims. Spending time with Catherine and our sons truly became my priority. As I realize now, that period and process encompassed a true passage to a higher stage of adulthood and was marked by an increased capacity for empathy and compassion. We all have a deep, and often unconscious, need to give ourselves to a higher purpose beyond self-interest. Those who can sublimate their needs and sacrifice for others, consistently and unconditionally, are among the most highly evolved adults.

Sometimes, however, sacrifice can be deceiving. There are versions of sacrifice that can be unhealthy, and here is where the importance of balance is so crucial. If sacrifice is driven by insecurity and fear or a distorted sense of responsibility for another's happiness, problematic patterns such as people-pleasing, caretaking, and enabling inevitably develop. These are also self-destructive versions of sacrifice. They are unconscious and maladaptive attempts to meet one's own needs for safety, security, love, belonging, and self-worth. These patterns are fed by faulty thinking exemplified by the beliefs that love, approval, and respect can be achieved by saying yes to everything; that stability can be maintained by compensating for another's problems or protecting others from negative consequences; or that you are responsible for sacrificing your own happiness for the sake of others. I've counseled men who embody these unhealthy patterns, but more often it is women who are most at risk for this type of self-deprivation, which never results in true need satisfaction. Initially, it may render an illusory sense of being loved and valued for your sacrifices, but, over time, people are apt to become dependent on those who do all the work, and usually offer little in return. The end result leaves the enabler with even more insecurity, fear, resentment, hurt, and burnout. I've observed countless examples of unhealthy sacrifice in my work:

- The wife of the alcoholic husband who calls in sick for him after a night of his binging, lies to her family and friends when he is unable to attend a gathering, and manages most housework and parenting
- The college student who drops everything for friends, even when it disrupts sleep, health and school work
- The woman who allows a needy friend to dominate her time with frequent calls and conversations about her problems
- The parents who exhaust themselves doing everything for their children, including things they should be learning to do for themselves
- The man who is burning out at work; he's always the first to pick up someone's shift, because he can't say no

When a child in a grown-up body makes a sacrifice for someone else, it is either for self-protection or it is conditioned on being rewarded with more love and approval. There is often indebtedness attached to the sacrifice. A score is being kept. When the adult makes a sacrifice for someone, it is an expression of empathy and compassion and the reward is the pleasure of seeing the other's need satisfied. Adults have learned to discern between sacrifices that are self-destructive and healthy. Adults make conscious choices that keep them in a healthy range of sacrifice. In adult relationships, there is a real sense of mutuality and partnership in that the participants are equally responsive to each other's needs. When I make sacrifices for other people, I feel like I'm making a good investment. I am investing in the well-being of people I care about; I am investing in the deepening of those relationships; I am investing in my own well-being; and I am investing in making the world a better place.

Practice this trait by thinking about people in your life and imagining yourself in their shoes. What might be their concerns? What needs might go unmet? What needs could be enhanced? What are some small but meaningful ways you might respond to their needs?

Using the scale from the "Ten Traits of the Adult," circle your
level of maturity related to the trait of sacrifice. Then identify a
growth goal and one or more specific steps you will begin to take.

You are pre-occupied   You balance equally
with your own needs and   making sacrifices for the
not responsive to other's   needs of others and
needs.   tending to your own valid
                                                            needs.

1……...…….2……………....3………….....4………...…5

Growth goal:

Specific steps:

TRAIT NINE

Competence

"In reading the lives of great men, I found that the first victory they won was over themselves. Self-discipline with all of them came first."

~ Harry S Truman

"I'm a great believer in luck, and I find the harder I work the more I have of it."

~ Thomas Jefferson

"Knowledge is power."

~ Sir Francis Bacon

"The winds and the waves are always on the side of the ablest navigators."

~Edward Gibbon

"In all things, success depends on previous preparation."

~ Confucius

Competence

I am developing the knowledge and skills that equip me for satisfying work, satisfying relationships, and independent living.

I often recommend a book by Susan Jeffers, that I've previously referenced, *Feel the Fear and Do It Anyway.* The author's basic premise is that we humans all have versions of worst case scenarios that can evoke strong fear and anxiety. She theorizes that fear is not the real problem, but rather, a core belief that if the worst did happen, we couldn't handle it. The book advocates our cultivating a core belief that we can deal with whatever we face in life including our worst case scenario – failure, rejection, loss. To believe we can handle life's challenges, we must have a core sense of competence – the belief, "I am capable." To be competent is to possess the knowledge and skills required to succeed in an endeavor. Just as insights are necessary tools for adulthood, so too are skills.

Imagine being magically transported to a completely foreign place. Everyone speaks your language, but beyond that, you have to start from scratch to provide for yourself, form all new relationships, and live independently. Although this could be stressful for anyone, the adult generally feels equipped to handle the challenge, whereas the child in the grown-up body might feel lost. Skills empower adults to adapt to change relatively well. For those who lack essential skills, change can be very intimidating.

Think about the myriad skills required to start over in a place unfamiliar to you. A few categories stand out – planning, organizing, job search, housing search, money management, vocational competencies, and interpersonal tools. These are the functional skills necessary for achieving true autonomy. I believe everyone needs to live independently, for at least a few years, to gain mastery over crucial life skills and build the confidence needed to succeed in the real world. Belief in our own competence is essential to being the adult in the room. Without this confidence, we opt for safety and dependence. All too often people stay in toxic relationships or jobs too long only because they don't believe they can create something better for themselves. I've witnessed grown-ups living chaotic lives due to disorganization, an inability to manage money, or lack of vocational skills. These kinds of incompetencies are incompatible with adulthood.

Not only do we need these skills in order to manage our lives, but we need the process of developing these tools to mature. **Think about what it takes to become competent in any pursuit:**

- A strong work ethic
- Assembling resources
- Commitment to a goal
- Setting priorities
- Persistent practice
- Time management
- Learning from mistakes
- Frustration tolerance and patience

When college students complain about having to take courses they will never use, I point out that their degree will not only be a reflection of the courses they took, but will also attest to their ability to demonstrate this list of strengths. The degree, in effect, is one measure of competence.

One of my favorite chapters in Malcolm Gladwell's bestselling book, *Outliers*, is entitled "The 10,000 Hour Rule." The chapter describes the true dedication to practice required to master a skill or craft and even goes so far as to identify an approximate amount of time spent practicing – ten thousand hours – to attain true mastery. Professional athletes provide the most obvious examples of this principle. Another example used by Gladwell is of the Beatles who played music in obscure nightclubs in Europe for years before they ever appeared on the world stage. They often played eight hour sets seven nights a week.

Overnight success is a myth. Successful people will tell you they built their success over a period of years with hard work, learning from countless mistakes and failures, and practice, practice, practice. For me, the term "private practice" has literal meaning. Every counseling session I've ever conducted has accounted for one of my ten thousand hours. With each hour I've learned, incrementally, the therapeutic insights and skills that equip me to be a competent therapist. With each upcoming session, I hope to continue to practice and learn.

A common issue in counseling is one's knowledge or skill deficiency in one or more areas of his life – interpersonal, organizational, parental, vocational, to name a few. Counseling doesn't do magic. If clients make progress, it's due in large part to their commitment to developing the knowledge and skills lacking.

Much of what I've previously addressed as adult traits can be framed as skill sets: cognitive skills, skills for dealing with feelings, and assertiveness skills. There are important life skills too numerous to mention, but I'm compelled to highlight two skill deficits that often surface as problems for clients – organization and listening.

Living a proactive and empowered life requires the ability to create order in our lives. I often see people who are controlled by impulses, living from one crisis to another in a constant state of reactivity and stress. For the most part, our degree of organization is a reflection of our personality and our learning. People who are wired for organization and who grew up in an ordered family system tend to create order in their lives intuitively, though this isn't always the case. People whose wiring predisposes them to inattention and impulsivity or who grew up in a chaotic family system, will likely have to learn and practice consciously the skills that bring order to their lives. Otherwise, the consequences of too much disorganization serve as barriers to achieving the level of competency required for adulthood. If you are in need of establishing more order in your life, there is an abundance of literature available to help you develop conscious strategies. Stephen Covey's book, *First Things First*, is one of my favorites.

The most important communication skill we can practice is active listening. It is the key to interpersonal competence and to developing close personal relationships. The most consistent theme in my work with clients who have relationship issues is their failure to listen skillfully. Listening is also the key to developing insight. If you look closely, you can observe the difference in maturity levels between those who are good listeners and those who are not. Because there are so many potential unconscious barriers, a unique level of self-awareness is required for effective listening.

We tend to associate communication with talking, but it is the quality of the listening that determines communication effectiveness. Listening starts with a conscious intention to truly understand the other person. Next, barriers need to be removed – being pre-occupied, being self-conscious, passing judgment, being defensive, needing to do the talking, needing to be right, and giving advice. Then, effort is made to understand the true meaning of the other's message through clarifying questions. Finally, understanding is conveyed through statements of validation or expressions of empathy.

I remember as a young therapist being self-conscious about whether or not I looked and sounded like a therapist and had credibility in the eyes of my clients. While I was preoccupied with what my clients thought of me, I was missing important information about what was happening to them. When I eventually resolved my own insecurities, I was able to listen to and understand my clients on a more effective level.

Because of the higher consciousness and inner security required to remove barriers to effective listening, the skill of listening is a measure of the highest level of adult functioning. There is abundant self-help literature dedicated to the full array of interpersonal skills including listening.

Take some time to reflect on your overall level of competence by rating yourself in the following categories and setting goals where needed along with specific, incremental steps you can take.

Work Ethic

       Rating: 1……..2………...3……...4………..5

       Goal:

       Specific steps:

Planning and Organizing Skills

       Rating: 1……..2………...3……...4………..5

       Goal:

       Specific steps:

Money Management

       Rating: 1……..2………...3……...4………..5

       Goal:

       Specific steps:

Time Management

Rating: 1……..2……...3……..4……….5

Goal:

Specific steps:

Vocational Skills

Rating: 1……..2……...3……..4……….5

Goal:

Specific steps:

Interpersonal Skills / Listening Skills

Rating: 1……..2……...3……..4……….5

Goal:

Specific steps:

Using the scale from the "Ten Traits of the Adult," circle your level of maturity related to the trait of competence. Then identify a growth goal and one or more specific steps you will begin to take.

| You have not acquired the knowledge and skills necessary to function competently in the adult world. | You have acquired the knowledge and skills necessary for satisfying work, satisfying relationships, and independent living |

.

1.….…..…..2.…………...3.………….....4.………...…5

Growth goal:

Specific steps:

Personal Growth

"The world breaks everyone, and afterward many are stronger in the broken places."

~Ernest Hemingway

"Experience is not what happens to you; it is what you do with what happens to you."

~ Aldous Husley

"If nothing is ventured, nothing is gained."

~ Sir John Heywood

"When the student is ready, the teacher will appear."

~Buddhist proverb

"Problems call forth our courage and our wisdom; indeed, they create our courage and our wisdom. It is only because of problems that we grow mentally and spiritually."

~ M. Scott Peck

"One can choose to go back toward safety or forward toward growth. Growth must be chosen again and again; fear must be overcome again and again.

~ Abraham Maslow

Personal Growth

*I am committed to new learning and growth and
I can take emotional risks.*

In my office hangs a framed cross-stitch Catherine made for me when I started my practice all those years ago. It's an image of a mature oak tree with the quote, "The only evidence of life is growth." Just seven simple words to capture my therapeutic philosophy. I often explain to clients that if they make progress, it won't come from a quick fix. Positive change is possible only through slow, subtle, incremental processes of new learning and growth.

There is an old saying, "The wiser you become, the more you realize how little you know." We all go through stages in our development when we seem to believe we know everything and have all the answers. Hopefully, we mature to a point we can easily admit how limited and flawed we are, how much we don't know, and how much we have to learn. It takes being secure with yourself to acknowledge when you've really blown something, made a mistake or don't know something, especially something everyone else seems to know. When you don't have to defend your ego, you are postured to grow, open to being influenced by new relevant information, and receptive to constructive feedback. You can take emotional risks.

Life is your curriculum. Life is always teaching. The real question is, do we have the mind-set to learn? There is truth in the old adage, "Problems are opportunities." Most of us can recognize that some of our darkest hours have taught us the most valuable lessons. For example, when I am working with a client who is dealing with clinical anxiety or facing cancer treatment or heart surgery, I am better equipped to be helpful since I've dealt with those same trials in my own life. Likewise, all of the ways I've been tested in my own marriage and in raising my own children have served my growth and enhanced my insight and empathy when working with couples and families. Now that I am in my sixties, I can see clearly the different stages that have posed unique challenges. Erich Erickson's model of what he called "psychosocial stages of development" has held true for my life. Erickson's model illustrates that each life stage presents a set of challenges and lessons to overcome to succeed in the world, to find peace and happiness, and prepare for the next stage. When we don't learn the lessons, we get stuck in our development.

The early stages of our life challenge us to build a sense of self and the competencies for independence, socialization, and work. The middle stages teach us about love, intimacy, sacrifice, patience, creativity, productivity, and purpose. The later stages have to do with regeneration, wisdom, loss, and mortality. When you see the series of stages in life, it's easy to see life as a journey. People overly focused on the destination tend to resist or miss what life is trying to teach them. Those who see themselves on the journey tend to be more receptive to the learning along the way.

Deeply religious clients, dealing with a life crisis, sometimes tell me they feel abandoned by God and disillusioned with their faith. They believed that if they did all the right things – regularly attended church, read their Bible, and prayed faithfully – God would protect them from hardship or quickly deliver them from it and now feel betrayed. I suggest that maybe God is found in the learning and growth we experience when we endure a crisis. Usually we have to weather the crisis before we can see the gain. Anyone who believes he is immune to adversity is headed for a hard fall, and anyone who can't tell you what he has learned from hardship has wasted invaluable experience.

At the highest level of adulthood we come to a spiritual understanding and appreciation for what it means to be living a life in process. We don't need to win a race or prove ourselves to anyone. We don't need to fight or control the challenges that distress us. We accept life on its own terms. There is gratitude for the whole of human experience – the joy in the good times and the growth from the hard times. At this level we are more adaptable in times of uncertainty and change. We are able to live more in the present and live more gracefully.

I'm an eternal optimist: I believe infinitely in our capacity to make changes based on our potential to learn. From the vantage point of helping people through dark times, I've been able to witness the power of the human spirit and its capacity for growth.

Albert Einstein famously said, "Insanity: doing the same thing over and over again and expecting different results." But what happens when you find the courage to make changes? Throughout my career, I have found, where there is the intention to learn, relationships heal, confidence is achieved, direction is found, independence is won, and goals are met in countless other ways.

- There was the young man, who at age fifteen was so out of control I worried he would wind up in jail. Now, at twenty-six, he has a college degree and a career in criminal justice.
- I worked with a young woman devastated by her divorce and dependent on her husband for security, identity, and self-worth. Now, several years later, she has a career and has a strong sense of self.
- I get holiday cards from the couple, once on the brink of divorce, who now look back on that very stressful time and see it, instead, a real turning point. They learned to understand and love each other on a deeper level.

- One particular young man was deeply dissatisfied with his career in the corporate world but found the courage and determination to go back to school to become a teacher. Today, he finds great joy in his work as a high school teacher and basketball coach.

- Another woman, who was overwhelmed with the sense of responsibility for the happiness of the people she loved, learned how to let go of the role of caretaker. Now, a few years later, there is a marked difference in her level of peace of mind.

- There was the father whose punitive approach to discipline hurt and alienated his children. He learned, through counseling and determination, to understand and respond to his children's needs and to discipline skillfully. Today, he enjoys a close relationship with his children.

Generally speaking, we don't achieve what we really want in life without taking emotional risks. Because we are instinctive beings, our lives are often controlled by our most powerful instinct: to safely stay with what we know, even if the known dissatisfies or even hurts us. For many children in grown-up bodies, the unknown, even with all its potential, is far scarier than a distressing known. The fear of failure or rejection stops millions of people in their tracks. This is a complicated issue. Taking risks, especially for the deeply insecure or those who lack basic competencies, can be a huge step. This is why many settle for lives of quiet desperation.

The only way to be an adult and meet higher-level needs is to risk failure and rejection. Successful people often acknowledge they endured many setbacks to accomplish their goals. Our capacity to be vulnerable and take emotional risks grows as we cultivate the foundational traits of self-acceptance, independent thinking, personal responsibility, positive core beliefs, basic competence, and assertiveness. These traits empower us to know and trust what we want. Moreover, they give us the confidence and ability to reach for what we want and the resilience to deal with those inevitable failures, rejections, and challenges along the way.

What I'm doing right now is a perfect example. I understand the slim odds of getting a book published. Perhaps common sense would tell me to stop writing immediately. But, to find the will to press on against the odds, I practice many of the traits I've addressed. My fundamental self-acceptance allows me to separate my self-worth from the probable rejections I may incur. And, of course, I certainly have had to trust my own thinking, my competence as a therapist, and what I've learned from my clients throughout my "10,000 hours." I've had to practice the self-talk that encourages me to trust myself and reminds me to let the outcome take care of itself and to value this process as much as the end result. There's no such thing as failure when you give something your best shot and learn from the experience. All of us have places in our lives that could be enhanced or even dramatically improved if we were to muster the courage to take the necessary risks.

One last old saying: "There is nowhere to get to and you're already there." Wherever you are on your journey is where you're supposed to be. Whatever is happening in your life is your curriculum, for now. The question is, "What is life trying to teach you?"

Do you need to learn more about who you are?

Is it time to develop a new skill?

What can you gain more insight about?

Can you accept something that is out of your control?

Do you need to leave an unhealthy environment?

Are you looking to find a new direction?

Are you ready to resolve feelings from the past?

Do you need to forgive someone?

Is now the time to make amends for something?

Have you put off grieving a loss?

What fear can you overcome?

Are you hungry for a creative challenge?

Could you be more proactive and resourceful?

Could you be more assertive?

Is it time to work on your patience?

Can you be more trusting of yourself? How about others?

Can you love more?

Is a nagging insecurity holding you back?

What's stopping you from taking a needed risk?

Is it time to cultivate new friendships?

Could you practice a healthier lifestyle?

Do you need to have more fun?

Are you ready to let go of assuming responsibilities for
everything and everybody?

Are you shirking responsibility in some area?

Could you be more responsive to the needs of the others
in your life?

Do you truly listen to those around you?

If there is something on this list that resonates with you, it is probably a signal it needs more attention. Embrace it as a growth goal. You can tackle any challenge with intention, consciousness, and practice. When you can identify a learning and growth goal, you are meeting one of the requirements for being the adult in the room.

Using the scale from the "Ten Traits of the Adult," circle your level of maturity related to the trait of personal growth. Then identify a growth goal and one or more specific steps you will begin to take.

You are focused primarily on   You value new learning and
safety and are risk avoidant.   growth and can take
                                                      emotional risks.

1………...……..2……………....3…………….....4…………...…..5

Growth goal:

Specific steps:

Two: The Adult in Marriage

". . . What of marriage, master?
And he answered saying:
. . . Aye, you shall be together even in the silent memory of God.
But let there be spaces in your togetherness,
And let the winds of the heavens dance between you.
Love one another, but make not a bond of love:
Let it rather be a moving sea between the shores of your souls.
Fill each other's cup, but drink not from one cup.
Give one another of your bread, but eat not from the same loaf.
Sing and dance together and be joyous, but let each one of you be alone,
Even as the strings of a lute are alone though they quiver with the same music.
Give your hearts, but not into each other's keeping.
For only the hand of Life can contain your hearts.
And stand together, yet not too near together:
For the pillars of the temple stand apart,
And the oak tree and the cypress grow not in each other's shadow."

~ Kahlil Gibran
The Prophet

Personal Responsibility Applied to Marriage

*I accept responsibility for helping create
a need-satisfying marriage.*

By the time Carl and Cindy entered counseling, Carl had a storehouse full of resentment toward Cindy and "one foot out the door." As is usually the case, their relationship was complicated. During their courtship, Carl served in the military and was considering making it his career. When Cindy expressed that the military lifestyle would be hard for her to accept, he chose, with mixed feelings, to leave the service after his tour of duty. Soon after his discharge, they married. In civilian life, Carl struggled to find a satisfying vocational niche, despite having no problem finding jobs. He soon found himself nostalgic for the sense of belonging and pride he experienced during his service days. Perhaps ironically, for a military person, he was passive, and took little initiative to explore options and deal proactively with his dilemma. Cindy, however, a take-charge personality, was playing a caretaker role and assuming the responsibility for motivating him to seek more gratifying employment and resolve his unhappiness. Together they unconsciously created a classic parent/child dynamic in their marriage. Cindy's sense of responsibility for Carl's happiness brought out in her what Carl viewed as her nagging him. He reinforced this pattern by deferring to her leadership and rarely asserting himself. All of this amounted to harbored resentment on both sides.

I discovered that Carl had always underachieved and had deep insecurities going back to his childhood. His time in the military had given him an illusory sense of identity, status, and belonging he could not provide for himself. The structure of the military also meant many decisions were made for him. When he left the service, these issues became exposed, yet Carl had convinced himself Cindy was to blame for his unhappiness. I was struck by how little personal responsibility Carl was taking and how much responsibility Cindy was assuming on his behalf.

Starting a marriage is a bit like working for an organization with no stated mission or vision. You have no job description and no prior orientation or training other than your dating experience and what you saw modeled in your parents' marriage, if there was one. It's hard to imagine someone truly prepared for marriage. If there was ever an example of "on the job training," marriage is it. I thought I was fairly mature and enlightened when I got married at the age of twenty-eight. After over thirty-five years of marriage, I realize how little I knew.

Out of this markedly undefined context, it should be no surprise that the marital dynamics and patterns that begin to evolve are usually more unconscious than conscious – hidden expectations, distorted perceptions, unresolved past issues, undeveloped identities, defensive communication, lack of insight about personality differences, and imprints from past learning. By now you've gotten my message that the fundamental difference between adults and children in grown-up bodies is the level of consciousness. Nowhere is our level of consciousness, and thus our degree of maturity, more revealed than in a marriage.

Normally, by the time couples come to counseling, they are so lost in their unconscious dynamics, it is difficult to untangle what has evolved. It's my challenge to completely re-orient them in an attempt to break entrenched patterns. The first step is to shift a couple's focus from negative feelings and behavior and refocus them on what marriage is supposed to be about.

The fundamental purpose of marriage is to create a relationship that enhances each partner's level of need satisfaction. This means we have to know what our needs are, know how to make them understood, and commit to be responsive to them. These needs, which I've addressed in earlier sections, are as follows:

- A basic sense of feeling safe and secure physically, emotionally, and materially
- Feeling loved and feeling a sense of closeness, intimacy, and belonging
- Feeling accepted, respected, affirmed, and valued
- Feeling a sense of partnership based on the mutual sharing of responsibilities and decision making
- Feeling empowered, supported, and encouraged to develop our potential and to pursue endeavors that give us a sense of higher purpose and meaning.

These needs lie just beneath the surface of every marital interaction. If they are relatively well satisfied, the relationship grows closer and stronger. When these needs are not satisfied, maladaptive patterns for meeting needs begin to form that can become powerful barriers to closeness and can ultimately destroy the relationship. When these needs are unmet, every interaction has the potential to trigger underlying hurt and anger.

Once I've reminded a couple that marriage is about meeting needs, I orient them to personal responsibility. Often, by the time couples enter counseling, they're stuck in a defensive cycle. Their responses to not having needs met have been communicated through their defenses so predominantly that they've hurt each other, often to the point that both partners feel like a victim of the other's malice. If this defensive cycle is allowed to continue, they'll eventually view each other as an enemy and the marriage will be destroyed. The defensive cycle cannot be broken until both partners recognize and claim their respective responsibility for creating and perpetuating the problems. Accepting personal responsibility is the first adult trait to practice if they are to make progress.

To begin to orient the couple to their responsibilities, I discuss with them the following points:

Marriage Responsibilities

- You are responsible for tending to your own physical, mental, and emotional wellness in order to be a healthy partner.
- You are responsible for getting your needs met in your marriage.
- You are responsible for developing self-awareness that allows you to identify consciously what you think, feel and need.
- You are responsible for asserting yourself rationally and respectfully in order to recruit your partner's understanding and help in meeting your needs.
- You are responsible for not allowing your hurt, anger and mistrust to build to a level that expresses itself reactively and destructively and for taking proactive steps to resolve your hurt, anger and mistrust constructively.
- You are responsible for deepening your understanding of your partner and his or her needs and for investing your time and energy in helping your partner satisfy needs.
- You are responsible for resolving issues such as personal insecurities, unusual neediness and dependency, wounds from childhood or previous relationships, and unresolved grief.
- You are responsible for not allowing distorted expectations, perceptions, and programming to become barriers to a healthy marriage.
- You are responsible for a commitment to personal growth that results in increased self-awareness, insight, knowledge, and skill that equip you to have a fulfilling marriage.

Fulfilling these responsibilities and creating a healthy marriage require both partners to practice all the other traits of adulthood. In this section I will explain how each trait is applied to a marriage. However, I don't address the trait of **competency** separately since this entire section is, in effect, about marital competency. Although I reference the context of marriage, the following principles and practices apply to all committed intimate relationships.

Self-Acceptance Applied to Marriage

*I am responsible for my own positive sense of self
and my own fundamental self-acceptance in my marriage.*

Beth and Sam began dating in their college years. Sam was two years ahead of Beth in school. By the time Sam approached graduation, they were in love and seriously committed to each other. They, like many young people, envisioned marriage as the next step after college and planned a wedding for shortly after Sam's graduation. Beth, who was unclear about her vocational direction, dropped out of school with two years remaining with the intention of finishing her degree after they settled into marriage. Soon, Sam became invested in his accounting career while Beth grew increasingly unfocused and restless about her life, yet also unmotivated to return to school. She turned her attention to having children to meet her need for purpose. By age thirty, Beth had three young children and was beginning to experience bouts of depression. She felt a nagging discontent and emptiness. Her deep insecurities led her to depend on her husband and children for her self-worth and happiness. There was a void in her life.

Beth was unconsciously deriving her sense of identity and self-worth from her role as wife and mother, and her lack of a deeper, more authentic sense of self had caught up with her. She rightly felt she had missed out on important experiences during her twenties. She was becoming aware of her passion and ability for interior design, but felt she'd missed her opportunity to return to school. Beth unknowingly skipped a crucial stage ideal for experiencing freedom, adventure, and "sowing wild oats" as well as for developing identity, independence, and direction.

I noted earlier the scientific studies that support that the human brain reaches physiological maturity at approximately age twenty-five. This, along with my own clinical observation, suggests to me that most of us have not achieved the level of mental and emotional maturity necessary to qualify us as good candidates for a marriage commitment until the latter half of our twenties at the earliest. Even then, there can be many reasons for our developmental age to be years younger. Sadly, I have worked with many couples who married before they knew who they truly were or what they wanted from life in adulthood only to realize, a few years into marriage, after maturing, they had made a big mistake.

Marie was raised by a verbally abusive father and grew up with some deep insecurities. Her relationships with men were marked by her attraction to dominant personalities and her need for their approval. She eventually married a handsome, charming, charismatic man whose attention made her feel attractive and important. "He was a real catch," as she put it. He placed a high value on image, but had very little substance. It was not long before his infidelity revealed the shallowness of their relationship and the marriage ended in divorce.

Knowing who we are and validating and accepting ourselves are cornerstones to being an adult. Whether or not individuals have this solid foundation can determine the outcome of a marriage. I've had clients admit they were literally charmed into getting married. They were, in a sense, drugged by the image projected by their spouse and his or her ability to make them feel worthy and appealing. When you're dependent on someone's charm to make you feel good about yourself, something is missing in you. If you enter marriage with the unconscious expectation that the marriage, and your association with your spouse, will give you self-worth and identity, you're already on the wrong track. You'll soon find yourself with an unhealthy orientation to what your spouse thinks and feels. You'll require too much affirmation and validation, and the affirmation you do receive will never be enough. You'll be overly vigilant about measuring how much you're valued and predisposed to mistrust and take personally the confusing signals and messages we all occasionally experience in marriage. You'll be unable to detach from your spouse's negative feelings and will instinctively interpret them as criticism of you. You'll perceive yourself as unvalued, which will lead to hurt and anger, and in turn, trigger defensiveness and conflict.

I was attracted to my wife for several reasons, but chiefly because she was secure with who she was. She lived independently, did her own thinking, and had a strong sense of purpose and direction for her life. Her wholeness meant she wasn't dependent on anyone for her happiness. I think inner security is the most attractive quality.

With a positive sense of self, comes a healthy differentiation between you and your spouse. You can assess realistically what your marriage and your spouse can and cannot do for you and what you have to do for yourself. You can enjoy the level of affirmation and validation that a healthy marriage should offer, and you can detach from the occasional bad moods and minor insensitivities that are inevitable. Unencumbered by insecurity, you carry more trust, peace, and happiness with you and contribute positive energy to the marriage.

As children, we were dependent on the affirmation of others to help us form our self-worth. When we find that someone's words or actions make us feel worthless or inferior, it suggests we've not outgrown that child-like dependence on outside approval. When a spouse has the power to make the other feel unacceptable, the whole dynamic will be distorted. My wife has the power to say or do something that could hurt me, but there is nothing she could say or do that could make me feel unacceptable. The same is true for her. When this is true for both of us, we don't have to waste emotional energy extracting from each other that which we do not have to give. We also are free from living in a state of angst when we don't need constant approval. When both individuals in a marriage have a positive sense of self, there is no undue pressure, mind-reading, mistrust, and over-vigilance toward each other. When self-acceptance resides within us, we're able to live in a relative state of peace and trust, allowing us to express the better parts of ourselves, which brings us closer.

If you are in a marriage and you don't have a good handle on who you are or on your self-acceptance, this insecurity is already causing problems, or it surely will. This is one of those core issues that can get lost amidst all of its symptoms. In a marriage, we have to learn how to distinguish between the symptoms and the real problem. If lack of self-acceptance is an issue for you, you are responsible for addressing and resolving this problem if you intend to be the adult in the room in your marriage. Refer back to "Self-Acceptance" in the first section and apply the exercises to your marriage.

Independent Thinking Applied to Marriage

I am responsible for doing my own thinking in my marriage.

Amy and Rick were appropriately nervous as they entered my office for the first time. After a few minutes of getting acquainted, I instructed them to each explain to me, while the other listened, their respective views of what had led up to them entering counseling. I asked each of them to identify their perception of the issues, themes, and patterns along with what they felt, wanted, and needed. I routinely begin my work with couples by asking them these questions. Not only am I listening for their answers, I am also observing their dynamic.

Rick volunteered to go first and began like a lawyer presenting his case before a judge. He was emphatic and self-righteous with a tone that lacked empathy toward Amy. Next, Amy spoke tentatively and seemed to be uncertain as to how she viewed their marital issues. While she was attempting to describe her perspective, she kept looking toward Rick with an approval-seeking expression, as if she needed his OK for what she thought. When I observed that she seemed to need Rick's approval for what she was expressing, she went silent for a moment and then said, "I guess I pay more attention to what he thinks than to what I think."

A mature marriage is comprised of two relatively well-formed and differentiated individuals. Another key ingredient to this healthy autonomy between partners is their ability to identify, trust, and be guided by their own thinking. This trait equips the individuals to engage fully in the marriage and to represent themselves well. This dynamic creates the potential for a couple to achieve a deep level of understanding and closeness. When one or both partners are not equipped with this trait, co-dependent patterns will likely develop. In a nutshell, co-dependency is a term for a relationship dynamic in which partners are too oriented to the other's thoughts, feelings, and needs and not oriented enough to their own.

A mature marriage strikes a balance between harmony (compatibility) and healthy tension (accountability). Partners need to be relatively compatible in terms of their most important values and beliefs; otherwise, they'll have too much conflict on a structural level, which is difficult to resolve. On the other hand, there needs to be freedom and safety in the marriage for both to express who they are by asserting what they think, particularly if they disagree. Partners are accountable for creating an environment that respects and encourages the expression of independent thought. This paves the way for a truly adult relationship because it leads to deeper levels of openness and honesty about who they are as individuals. Over the course of a marriage, we as individuals change as we grow. If we are growing, aspects of our worldview change, elements of our philosophy change, our view of ourselves changes, usually some of our priorities change, and what we want or envision can change. We have to know and to express what's happening within us if we are to show up fully in marriage. Marriage should be the place where we feel the safest to explore and to express the deepest levels of our being with another. If one or both partners are not oriented enough to their own thinking and its validity, then one will take too many cues from the other and distort the whole dynamic. Without this healthy independence, the assertiveness needed to maintain mutual accountability is lost and will lead to an inevitable power imbalance.

Many marriages are marked by the dominance of one partner's strong will due to the other partner's lack of independent thinking and inability to stand his or her own ground. In other cases, partners have acknowledged they didn't know each other very well, sometimes after being together for years, because they lacked the depth inherent in independent thought required to communicate below the surface of their relationship. These marriages may be functional, but they fall short of being mature, intimate marriages.

If you are in a marriage and unable to express or assert what you think on a depth level because you don't know or trust your own thinking, then your marriage is at risk as well as your own mental and emotional well-being. Independent thinking is a key to getting your needs met and a key to deepening your relationship. If this is an issue for you and you intend to have a mature marriage, you're responsible for making independent thinking a priority for your personal growth. Refer back to "Independent Thinking" in the first section, and apply the exercises to your marriage.

Conscious Feeling Applied to Marriage

I process and manage my feelings consciously in my marriage.

I had worked with Molly and Ben long enough to open our session with this question: "Has anything occurred this week between you two that we can use for practice?" Ben spoke up to report things were going much better and he couldn't think of any problems from the week. I turned to Molly who awkwardly looked at Ben and said, "What about last night?" Ben confusedly asked, "What do you mean?" Molly reminded Ben that when he came home from work last night and found her in her home office, instead of greeting her kindly, he asked in a harsh and sarcastic tone, "Is that all you're going to do tonight is work!?" and then retreated to the den. Molly felt so stung by the tone of his comment that she withdrew and hardly spoke to him for the rest of the evening.

This episode was a microcosm of the defensive loop in which they were stuck, but to their credit they were both able to examine the episode non-defensively. Ben observed that last night seemed so normal to him that he couldn't even recognize it as a problem. He gave Molly credit for bringing it up because ordinarily she would repress her feelings and stay withdrawn from him. As we peeled back the layers, here is what was really going on under the surface:

- Ben loves Molly and wants to feel closer to her, but his perception is that she loves her work more than she loves him. Sometimes he feels unloved and rejected by Molly. He had hopes of some quality time with her last night but when he saw her working, it triggered his feelings of disappointment and rejection and thus his defensive jab at her. We agreed that when Ben saw her working, he needed to have the consciousness to simply say, "I was hoping I could have some time with you tonight."

- Molly loves Ben and wants to feel closer to him, but his defensive reactions have hurt her. She withdraws when she's hurt. When she represses her feelings and withdraws from him, he has no way of knowing how much he hurts her, and her withdrawal feeds his perception that she doesn't love him. Molly loves her work, but she loves Ben more. When she feels disconnected from Ben, she immerses herself in her work. Last night she had the intention of stopping work when Ben got home so they could spend time together. She would have loved to hear Ben tell her he was hoping to have some of her time. We agreed that after Ben took his jab at her last night, rather than withdraw, she needed to be able to say to him, "That really hurt. What was that about?"

Much of the dynamic in a marriage turns on how the partners handle their feelings, particularly the negative ones. In a childish marriage, unconscious, unmanaged feelings become weapons. I have watched in amazement as partners say horrible things to each other and feel justified in doing so because they were offended or hurt. Every marriage is at risk to develop the "defensive cycle" when we're not processing and managing our feelings consciously. One's defensive reaction offends or hurts the other, triggering the other's defensive reaction. With each volley, the ante is upped until, sometimes, irreparable damage is done. All the while, the real issue is lost, if it was ever identified to begin with. If this defensive cycle is allowed to continue for even a brief period, it will likely damage the two pillars of marriage – trust and respect. Trust is the belief that my partner, who may inadvertently hurt me due to insensitivity or defensiveness, truly has my best interests at heart and would never intentionally or maliciously hurt me. Respect is the belief that my partner fundamentally respects who I am. If one or both partners begin to believe that the other has true malicious intent or no longer respects the other, the marriage is in trouble.

I'm struck sometimes by how high-functioning we can be in most parts of our lives, but how quickly we can regress to a childish level in our marriage. Yet, this phenomenon does make some sense when you stop and think. Where else do we live with someone as intensely day in and day out with our most powerful needs at stake? Marriage is the place that presents us with the most material for conflict and misunderstanding. There aren't many things on the planet more complex than a marriage of two human beings.

Because of the countless ways humans can misunderstand one another, there is abundant potential for us to evoke in each other frustration, irritation, confusion, disrespect, hurt, sadness, loneliness, fear, worry, anger, resentment – just to name some basics. Now add to these energies the array of negative feelings that we sometimes bring home from the outside world that we can unconsciously infuse into our marriage. We have our work cut out for us to be the adult in the room when processing and managing feelings in marriage.

I had a session recently with Sandy and Brent, for whom I have a real affinity and respect. Despite the fact they're both intelligent, accomplished, professional people, they have a way of bringing out the child in each other. This is the second marriage for both, and each brings some family of origin issues with them. Sandy's defenses tend towards the aggressive and Brent's towards the passive. There are times when Brent feels resentment toward Sandy for what he perceives as her nagging and criticizing. When he finally expresses his pent-up resentment, he calls her "Alice," the name of his ex-wife, for whom he feels only contempt. There is probably nothing he could say that could be more disrespectful and hurtful. Sandy's response is to tell him that when he calls her Alice, she "hates his guts." So, here are two people systematically destroying the pillars of trust and respect because they are failing to process and manage their feelings consciously.

Both Sandy and Brent need to identify their vulnerable feelings underneath the anger and resentment and talk to each other rationally and respectfully about what one is doing that causes the other to feel hurt and disrespected. Then, they have to be able to explain what they need from the other in order to feel more loved and respected.

Cheryl lost her mother at an early age; her father was cold and detached. She grew up feeling abandoned and unloved. These primal feelings were still unresolved when she married Richard, a good man who loved her but whose pattern of people-pleasing prevented him from setting healthy boundaries with other family members and his ex-wife. The effects of this pattern often left Cheryl feeling she was not a priority and hence, once again, abandoned and unloved. These feelings would build in her to a boiling point. Then, an incident would trigger an eruption of anger that sometimes could spew for days.

Cheryl had valid complaints and feelings about Richard's lack of boundaries, particularly with his ex-wife. However, these episodes would trigger her deeper unresolved anger from childhood that was out of proportion to his offense and also out of her control. When we processed this, Cheryl explained that during those eruptions, she needed Richard to hold her, comfort her, and reassure her that he loved her and that everything would be OK. In effect, Cheryl was saying that she could not manage her own feelings at those times and that she needed Richard to calm her like a nurturing parent would respond to a child's meltdown.

In subsequent episodes, Richard attempted to respond as she requested, but it didn't work. The problem was that during her meltdown she was saying extremely harsh things to him, while wanting him to hold and comfort her. Nothing has more power to scare off and shut down a people-pleaser than angry disapproval.

It would take an unusually secure person to do what she was asking. We came to the conclusion that it was unreasonable for Cheryl to expect Richard to move closer to her at those times, unless she could make it safer for him by managing her feelings better. Repressed feelings from the past must be identified and managed consciously, otherwise they can wreak havoc on a marriage.

Untangling Cheryl's and Richard's patterns was a challenge. Richard needed to work on being more assertive and setting healthier boundaries that reflected his wife as his top priority. Cheryl had to explain her needs to him more clearly and make specific requests in order to get her love needs met. She had to learn to distinguish between feelings related to the present and repressed feelings from the past, and she had to learn how to keep those feelings separate and express them constructively.

In the early years of my marriage, I would find myself annoyed with Catherine because I had no tolerance for clutter. Catherine is a teacher, and most teachers, particularly the creative ones, tend to carry a lot of stuff with them. She had a habit of bringing her stuff home and putting it down on any available surface where it would linger, spread out and eventually pile up. The longer this pattern continued, the more annoyed I became. I viewed the clutter judgmentally, and I also interpreted it as an act of disrespect and took it personally – all distortions. I then began to take disrespectful pot shots at her when I would feel the annoyance.

I eventually realized my annoyance was my issue and I was responsible for making myself better understood and for asking for what I needed. After processing more consciously what my annoyance was really about, I was able to explain that my personality is hopelessly hard-wired for order and that a certain amount of clutter stresses me. I asked her to be understanding of how clutter affects me. She, in turn, had a valid request of me to work on being less compulsive and more flexible, which I honored. As a result of discussing the issue rationally and respectfully and working together to solve the problem, we long ago resolved this misunderstanding and conflict. Now, if her stuff accumulates, I'm more accepting. And because she understands that clutter stresses me and observes my increased flexibility and lack of criticism, she willingly is mindful of the clutter. The key to us solving this problem relied on my ability to go beyond my defensive feelings and identify the core feeling – stress – at the root of the problem and to recruit her help.

One of the most important steps I've learned to practice as I process feelings in my marriage is to ask myself, "Is this feeling about small stuff or big stuff?" Most negative feelings in a marriage consist of frustration, annoyance, and irritation. These feelings usually relate to small stuff – differences in personality, cultural and learning differences, individual quirks, minor insensitivities, or someone's bad day. Small stuff is inconsequential, and the frustration due to small stuff is a price we have to pay to live in a marriage. I often emphasize to clients that marriage is more about what we have to accept in the other than what we should expect the other to change. Therefore, when I ask myself, "Is this about small stuff or big stuff?", if the answer is small, I choose to accept it. When I reach this conclusion, I can usually resist the temptation to say something, but in some situations, I still need to express my frustration as I let go.

If you often feel unloved or lonely or experience chronic hurt, fear, disrespect, despair, or resentment, you're squarely in the "big stuff" category and you're responsible for connecting the dots to these feelings and addressing the issue with your partner as soon as possible. I've witnessed one spouse inform the other of longstanding unhappiness and readiness to end the marriage as the other listened in shock because this was the first time he or she was being told the extent of these feelings.

Many grown-ups have difficulty effectively identifying and expressing feelings in the "big stuff" category. Without this essential skill, we're left with only fight or flight reactions to express negative feelings. An accurate vocabulary is required to articulate the vulnerable feelings underneath our defenses. Ahead is an array of feeling words that describe some of our most vulnerable emotions. If any of these words describe feelings you experience on a recurring basis, you're responsible for preventing them from building up by addressing them assertively. If you do not identify with these words, then you and your marriage are probably in good shape.

hurt	mistrustful	embarrassed	discouraged
unloved	abandoned	helpless	inadequate
alone	disrespected	ashamed	guilty
rejected	disconnected	worthless	anxious
confused	afraid	sad	resentful
betrayed	overwhelmed	hopeless	disappointed

If you experience any of the above feelings, use the following "I-message" technique to frame and to express them rationally and skillfully to your spouse.

I feel _____ when _____, because _____.

Examples:

- I feel rejected when we're with your family because they focus totally on you and seem to make no effort to relate to me.

- I feel anxious when clutter accumulates because I'm hard-wired for order.

- I feel disrespected, betrayed, and resentful when you criticize me in front of our friends because I believe our complaints with each other should be reserved for our private conversation.

- I feel abandoned when you spend most of the weekend playing golf because spending time with me doesn't seem to be a priority for you.

Negative feelings in a marriage have the potential to serve an important purpose when we process them and manage them consciously. They can act as signals that inform us of our deeper needs and whether or not they're getting met. If we're able to connect our negative feelings to our deeper needs and to make ourselves understood to our spouse, we can view the feeling as a symptom and meeting the need as the cure.

In order to take responsibility for processing and managing your feelings as an adult in your marriage, revisit the trait of "Conscious Feeling" in the first section and apply the recommended questions to your marriage. The upcoming section on "Assertiveness in Marriage" will further elaborate on this topic.

Positive Core Beliefs Applied to Marriage

I consciously choose thoughts and beliefs
that enhance the quality of my marriage.

W e have approximately sixty thousand thoughts a day, give or take a few thousand. The world and the marriage we live in are created through the prism of these thoughts and beliefs. And, no doubt, people who think positively are much more equipped for the challenge and responsibility of marriage than those who let negative thoughts and beliefs undermine their peace and happiness. Distorted thinking is at the root of many marital problems. Negative programming can manifest itself in insecurities, neediness, mistrust, defensiveness, and faulty perceptions and expectations that ultimately lead to stressful marital dynamics. The way we think brings out either the best or the worst in us.

Two truths explain why our mental programming is such a powerful force in our lives: Our perception becomes our reality, and our thoughts and beliefs become self-fulfilling prophecies. Therefore, we must not leave the nature of our thinking to chance. There are certain types of thoughts and beliefs we must practice consciously in order to succeed in marriage. Below are five categories of thought and belief that strongly influence the outcome of a marriage:

> Self-worth
> Empowerment
> Trust
> Expectations
> General Attitude toward Life

Pay attention to the affirmations I've attached to each of these categories because they speak to the heart of what we must practice and believe in order to succeed in marriage.

Self-worth: **I am worthy of love and respect.**
I am a loving person capable of giving love.

The principle known as "the law of attraction" asserts that we all send signals that both attract us to and attract to us the people and experiences that align with our unique programming. These signals are like a dog whistle transmitted on a subliminal frequency. For example, insecure people in need of outside approval send people-pleaser signals that attract strong-willed people to whom they surrender their power. People who need to be needed to feel worthy and loved send caretaker signals that attract needy people with problems who have little to give. Sometimes opposite personalities attract because we see traits in the other that we feel we lack, and our association with the other gives us an illusory sense of wholeness. There are a hundred different versions of the law of attraction but, in general, children in grown-up bodies experience attractions driven primarily by unconscious forces. Adult attraction functions on a relatively high level of consciousness regarding what is right and healthy for each partner. If you subscribe to the law of attraction, it's easy to see how the core beliefs we transmit can set the tone and the direction for a marriage.

If you believe you're worthy of love and respect, you'll be attracted to people who are capable of being responsive to your needs and you'll be intolerant of too much insensitivity. If you believe you're less than worthy of love and respect, you're more likely to be attracted to people who have little to give and you'll tolerate too much hurt and disrespect. If you're insecure about your worth, you'll be predisposed to negative perceptions that will trigger defenses. You'll then transmit negative energy that will attract negative responses. The more secure you are with yourself, the less you'll rise and fall based on what your flawed spouse does and says, enabling you to take minor insensitivities in stride. Your inner security transmits positive energy that attracts your partner's love and respect.

When you believe yourself to be a loving person capable of giving love, you have confidence that you have much to offer a marriage. That confidence opens you to learning how to increase your capacity to love and to express love effectively. Quite naturally, the giving of love attracts your partner's love to you. When you believe yourself to be less than a loving person who has little to give, your sense of inadequacy with your attendant defenses inhibits your expression of love. As your partner feels unloved, you attract defensively expressed hurt and anger. Simply stated, the law of attraction means if you want to be respected and loved in your marriage, believe in your own worth, lovability and capacity to be loving. Then, expect to be treated with love and respect as well as give love and respect.

Empowerment: **I can assert myself to get my needs met.**
I can deal with challenges in my marriage proactively.
I focus on what is within my control.

Another belief about ourselves that impacts a marriage has to do with our sense of empowerment. A healthy marriage achieves a balance of power in which both partners have influence over decisions and can shape their environment to satisfy their needs. There is mutual accountability and a sense of equal partnership.

This balance of power is not achieved by accident; it requires two adults who believe themselves capable of the assertiveness necessary to stand up for themselves and make themselves understood. Empowerment means you believe you can deal with most anything in life and overcome most obstacles. Those who live empowered lives live proactively, focused on what is within their control, rather than dwelling on what they can't control. Empowered people bring positive energy to a marriage and address issues constructively to keep the marriage on the right track. If one or both partners come to the marriage with core beliefs such as "I'm powerless," "I'm a victim," or "I can't deal with it," they are likely to avoid addressing tougher issues and allow problems to build to an irreparable point. A sense of powerlessness also breeds underlying resentments that can contribute to a marriage's demise.

Trust: **I consciously practice trusting my partner's love, commitment, and intention toward me.**

Another crucial category of belief involves trust. People who grew up in an abusive or neglectful environment or who were abused or betrayed in previous relationships are predisposed to mistrust the intentions of a spouse. I believe most people are good, with positive intentions, and aren't going to hurt me. This belief equips me to enjoy the security found in trusting Catherine's love and commitment, even when in conflict. When I'm left with only perceptions to go on, I consciously choose to trust Catherine has my best interests at heart. There are those who bring into their marriage the unconscious belief that people can't be trusted and project this mistrust onto their spouse. When there's conflict, they perceive their partner to have malicious intent, which compounds the problem. They look for evidence to twist to confirm their mistrust. This dynamic creates unnecessary hurt and anger. We have to consciously practice trusting thoughts and beliefs in marriage. I'm not, however, suggesting blind trust. Certainly we need to see evidence of a partner's love and commitment.

Elaine's father openly cheated on her mother throughout her childhood. When Elaine entered her own marriage with Brandon, she did so with an unconscious, but powerful, belief that men can't be trusted to be faithful. Brandon's work required him to travel. When he left town, Elaine would immediately imagine him cheating on her. When he would call her at night, their conversations would be marked by her suspicions and, at times, accusatory tone. She'd seek the smallest detail on which to question him. Since I was counseling both of them, my sense was Brandon was truly committed to her. It was her mistrust that was damaging their marriage. Elaine was not conscious of how much her primitive mistrust was controlling her. With higher consciousness, she was able to practice trust by focusing on the abundant evidence of Brandon's love and commitment which helped quiet her inner voice of mistrust.

Expectations: **I consciously practice healthy and realistic expectations in my marriage.**

Our expectations of a marriage require consciousness. If our vision of romance and marriage has been influenced by Hollywood and Madison Avenue, we are bound to be disappointed and possibly disillusioned with a real-life marriage. Love doesn't make us mind-readers, and the love of a spouse doesn't give us wholeness and bliss. We can expect a marriage to enhance the quality of our lives, but marriage doesn't solve our problems.

We all enter marriage with unconscious images, expectations, and beliefs about how marriage should look and operate. Unconscious expectations have their origins in the models of marriage and family witnessed during childhood. This imprint, made during formidable years, is so powerful we are at risk to unconsciously recreate those models, regardless of whether they were positive or negative. Family systems theory suggests that this imprint is comprised of the following five elements that are modeled in every family:

- Roles: husband/wife and parent/child
- Rules to live by: beliefs, values, priorities
- Boundaries
- Patterns of communication
- Distribution of power

Imagine the potential for conflict when spouses' unconscious, imprinted models and expectations collide. Consider these examples:

- Roles: The wife's father had a stable, lucrative career with which he provided her family a comfortable life style. Her mother never had to work. The husband's parents both had to work to make ends meet. The husband has struggled to find his career path. He has changed jobs several times, resulting in meager incomes. She unconsciously judges him for not being as good a provider as her father. He resents her for not shouldering the burden with him.

- Rules to live by: One partner grew up in a family that stressed the principles of hard work, being productive, and not wasting time. The other spouse's family believed life is to be enjoyed and frequently made plans for fun and adventure. In marriage the partners unconsciously judge the other's priorities.

- Boundaries: A wife who is very close to her parents expects her husband to support her desire to have frequent contact with her parents. The husband, who is not close to his divorced parents, does not place a high priority on time with family. He resists frequent contact with her extended family. He sees his wife as dependent on her parents; meanwhile, she resents her husband for not valuing the parental bond.

- Patterns of Communication: The wife grew up in a family that openly expressed love, affection, and affirmation. The husband grew up in a family in which there was little to no expressed love, affection, and affirmation. She often feels hurt because he never hugs, compliments, or tells her he loves her. He thinks everything is fine because love is assumed.

- Distribution of Power: The husband's father made all of the financial decisions in his family. The wife grew up with a divorced single mother who effectively managed the finances. The husband tends to make key financial decisions without consulting his wife when she expects to be involved. They often argue about money.

The collision of unconscious expectations can turn into power struggles as partners attempt to establish the way of life to which they are accustomed. The longer these power struggles last, the more disconnected partners become. Ultimately, the solution requires both to loosen their grip on their expectations and together formulate a conscious and healthy set of expectations.

General Life Attitude: **I help create positive energy in my marriage by consciously focusing on the positives.**

One last category of conscious thought in marriage relates to one's ability to think positively in general. A mature marriage commitment includes a responsibility to help create a positive environment within which to live. Because life can be stressful, we have to choose consciously to focus more on the positive than negative. People who look for good news in situations and people have more successful marriages than those who think negatively. These partners buoy and encourage the other and, in doing so, create a buffer zone from stresses in the outside world. Their positive energy helps create an uplifting environment. Because they focus more on the positive, they more naturally communicate affirmation, gratitude, and optimism.

People who think negatively create a danger zone around themselves. Because they're more focused on the negatives, they naturally communicate criticism, ingratitude, and pessimism. Rather than buffer a partner's stress from the outside world, they add to it.

Familiarity in marriage can insidiously desensitize us to the qualities in our spouse that we were attracted to and fell in love with, in the first place. We can take for granted the many little things we do for each other each day. My marriage is typical in that I could allow the small stuff to chronically irritate me if I didn't practice positive thinking. I'm analytically wired. Analytical thinking is critical thinking and tends to focus on the flaws. I learned a long time ago how to talk myself through my irritations by reminding myself of all of the things that I love, admire, and appreciate about Catherine. I remind myself of what it must take for her to tolerate me at times. As I process these thoughts consciously, my irritation dissolves and is replaced by a renewed sense of love and respect for her.

Thoughts and beliefs about ourselves, trust, expectations, empowerment, and our general level of positive or negative thinking are powerful forces in a marriage. Marriages tend to succeed or fail based on the partners' abilities to consciously practice healthy, positive thoughts and beliefs in these categories. Remember the principle that thoughts and beliefs become self-fulfilling prophecies. If there are problems in your marriage, first check your thinking. The chances are high that one or both of you have gotten lost in faulty perceptions and distorted thinking. Don't hesitate to get counseling. A good cognitive therapist can help you sort out your thinking.

Insight Applied to Marriage

I practice insights that equip me to have a healthy marriage.

One of the many recurring arguments Paul and Heather had was about their dining room table. Paul had a habit of putting stuff on the table and leaving it there. Seeing his stuff on the table drove Heather crazy. She would call him a slob and he would dismiss her as being anal. To Paul, what was on the dining room table was no big deal. To Heather, how the table looked was a very big deal.

I asked them to describe their respective dining rooms during their childhood. They both chuckled at what they considered to be a strange question, but their answers surprised them, and I could see the light bulbs come on as they spoke.

Paul grew up in a small house and his father, who was a university professor, used the dining room as his study. He remembered a dining room table covered with books and papers. Heather's childhood dining room was "museum-like," as she put it. It was rarely used for meals; its purpose was primarily for show. She described an ornately decorated dining room table that was kept in perfect order.

Imagine now the countless little unconscious imprints from our childhood with which we enter a marriage.

In the previous section, I suggested that many marital conflicts stem from distorted thinking. Now I would suggest that much of that faulty thinking stems from lack of insight. You can't be the adult in the room in your marriage without adequate insight. It's just too easy, otherwise, to misinterpret your partner. It is human instinct, after all, to feel threatened by what we don't understand. The more we understand a problem, even though we may continue to disagree with or dislike it, the less defensive and more equipped we are to deal with it constructively.

Let's start with the premise that most of what occurs in your marriage and the ways in which you and your partner behave make perfect sense, even when the dynamic and the behavior seem inexplicable. In the first section on the adult trait of insight, I posited that four elements explain most human behavior: level of need satisfaction, learning, personality, and emotions. Let's now apply each of these insights to marriage.

Needs: **Yours and your partner's behavior is often related to valid needs.**

The driving force in our lives is need satisfaction. Ideally, we draw on a variety of resources for the enhancement of our needs: ourselves, family, friends, work, faith community, hobbies, along with our marriage. It's unrealistic to expect our marriage to be our only resource, but it is realistic to expect marriage to be a core resource. If a negative dynamic or negative behavior patterns develop in your marriage, the first question to ask is "What needs are unmet?" The following statement is a general template for connecting negative behavior patterns and needs:

Most negative behaviors in marriage are defensive behaviors, somewhere on the continuum between fight and flight. Defenses are triggered by a perceived threat. Although defensive behavior can injure, its primary purpose is self-protection. On rare occasions, one's physical safety feels threatened. In most marriages, the perceived threat relates to psychological/emotional safety in which needs for acceptance, love, intimacy, respect, affirmation, and empowerment feel threatened. Each partner has a dominant defensive style. Some people are more prone to attack and others are more prone to withdraw. A couple can get lost in the defensive cycle and do damage before they know it. With this insight, partners can recognize, sooner than later, what is happening and shift the focus to talking about what each needs.

The following are scenarios in which unmet needs lead to a defensive cycle that goes too far:

- A wife feels unloved and neglected by her husband and compensates by becoming enmeshed with their children. Her husband perceives being excluded and withdraws from family life.
- An insecure husband so fears losing his wife that he is constantly suspicious and questioning her whereabouts and who she's with. In an effort to protect herself, she over-reassures him and begins to be less than honest to prevent him from distorting innocent information and using it against her.
- A husband often looks for excuses to work late at his office because he fears going home to his wife's criticism. His wife feels abandoned when he works late and expresses her hurt through criticism.
- A wife exhibits an overbearing care-taking pattern driven by needs for security and love. Her husband becomes overly dependent on her but resents and blames her for how powerless he feels.
- A wife feels unloved and undesired by her husband and has an affair. Her husband is devastated by the betrayal and ends the marriage.

Early in my marriage a pattern developed in which I would examine our credit card bill and then interrogate Catherine about many of the charges. My tone had an edge of mistrust, criticism, and disrespect. For good reason, Catherine was mildly defensive, but restrained, when she had good reason to tell me where I could stick the bill! She was as conservative with money as I was. We were doing OK financially and managing our money well, so what was this issue really about for me?

I eventually was able to connect the dots and discuss the issue with Catherine on the need level, which allowed me to break my defensive pattern of mistrust and criticism. Like many men of my generation, I felt primarily responsible for providing for our family financially, while also harboring a deep fear of going broke. I was able to explain to Catherine how much I worried about money at times and the significance of my need to feel secure financially. I explained that unfamiliar purchases and carrying credit card debt triggered my fears. I had to recognize that her purchases were as valid as mine. They were just different. Most importantly, I needed to trust that she shared the sense of financial responsibility with me and that we both felt accountable to each other when spending our money. Ever since that conversation, we've done a great job of discussing our purchases, consulting each other on significant ones, and voluntarily informing each other about the smaller but confusing ones. For years now, I've had my need for financial security met by knowing I have a true partner when it comes to managing our money. Sometimes I think about how easy it would have been for me to have continued to express my need defensively and the damage that would have done over time. The next time you encounter confusing or negative behavior from your spouse, before you allow it to trigger your defenses, consider if the behavior might reflect an unsatisfied need.

Learning: Behavior is often explained by learning.

Much of our behavior reflects our learning. I believe that most of us are doing the best we know how, given what we've learned. We are powerfully imprinted by our models of marriage and family life, and we each bring these frames of reference into our marriage, often unconsciously. Again, when we encounter a spouse's behavior that confuses or distresses us, an early question to ask is, "Might this behavior reflect my partner's learning?" Remember, we can deal with the behavior better if it makes sense; otherwise, we'll likely misinterpret its meaning. The elements of a family system that I used in the previous section to explain unconscious expectations can also be the framework for understanding the prior learning we bring to a marriage. Here again are those elements:

- Roles: husband/wife and parent/child
- Rules to live by: beliefs, values, priorities
- Boundaries
- Patterns of communication
- Distribution of power

If we look closely at a marriage, in most cases, we can recognize the resemblance between each spouse's behavior patterns and how their respective families functioned in these categories. When someone's model was healthy and positive, they usually are ahead of the marriage learning curve, and where it was unhealthy and negative, they have extra ground to make up. It's irrelevant, however, as to where each spouse is on the learning curve as long as both are committed to consciously learning what is required of a healthy marriage. Here are a few examples of how the collision of prior learning experiences can explain some marital conflict.

- Joe never saw his father lift a finger to help around the house; and, likewise, it never occurs to him to help with housekeeping chores. Sarah's father and mother shared housekeeping responsibilities, and she views Joe as lazy.
- Rita was micro-managed while growing up and was told how to think and what to do. She didn't learn how to make decisions. She defers constantly to Chris and then resents him for having all of the control.
- Mary was over-indulged as a child and given whatever she wanted. She had no concept of how to manage money. She continues to make impulsive purchases and creates financial stress in her marriage.
- In Sue's family, conflict was met with arguing and yelling. In Gary's family, conflict was avoided and feelings were repressed. Neither of them know how to deal with conflict constructively.

- Allison played a caretaker role in her troubled family growing up. She doesn't know how to identify and validate her own needs and how to let go of assuming so much responsibility for everyone else. Her worries and anxiety create stress in her marriage.
- Lou grew up in a family that expressed little to no love, affection, and affirmation. Rhonda grew up in a family in which expressions of love flowed. She often feels unloved.
- Art was the only child in his family; he enjoyed privacy and never had to learn how to share. Katie was one of five children; she had no privacy and shared practically everything. Art was extremely territorial, while Katie had little awareness of personal space.
- With Luke's parents, debt was a way of life. They didn't deprive themselves of something they wanted, even if they couldn't afford it. Maintaining an image was part of the value system. Linda's parents stressed living within their means, saving for the future, and spending on the basis of need. Their values and spending habits often collided.

These are but a few examples of how prior learning can explain the way partners function in a marriage and how conflicting patterns cause frustration. When we can perceive that our partner's otherwise confounding behavior makes sense because it was learned, we're less likely to judge it, take it personally, and be defensive, and we're more likely to be patient and accepting.

Children in grown-up bodies respond to these conflicts by engaging in power struggles, with each defending his or her own way of life. The mature response is for each spouse to examine his or her respective patterns compared to healthy models, with an openness to acknowledging flaws, jointly creating a conscious vision, and learning new skills. In some marriages, creating healthy patterns may require a major overhaul, but it can be done when partners are willing to learn. It is often a revelation when partners realize they are unconsciously reenacting patterns learned in childhood. This insight leads to more openness to new learning.

As you attempt to increase your understanding of your spouse, ask yourself, "What behaviors might be explained by learning or the lack thereof?" Apply these same questions to your own behavior patterns. Together, create a vision of the patterns that you want and commit yourselves to learning the new skills.

Personality: Behavior is often a reflection of personality.

Rarely do I work with a couple in therapy whose conflict is not explained, in part, by their personality differences and a lack of insight about each other's inherent traits. On most days, we're just being who we are, based on our personality. Yet spouses with enough opposing traits find countless ways to judge the other's differences or interpret them as assaults. Again, our first instinct is to feel threatened by what we don't understand. Therefore, when you don't understand your partner's behavior, stop and consider that the behavior might be a natural expression of your partner's valid personality traits and not aimed at you. How personality explains most behavior is an essential insight in marriage.

Our personality traits exist on a continuum between opposites. Obviously, couples who have similar traits usually understand each other better than those whose traits are highly divergent. I see consistent marital problems among couples whose traits fall on opposite ends of the spectrum. These couples must practice exceptional insight and consciousness to avoid the misunderstandings and conflicts that can so easily arise due to their opposite personalities.

Here are a few of the most common themes I observe in conflict among couples whose traits are dramatically different.

Extraversion or Introversion

- The extraverted spouse is typically more driven to engage and interact than the introverted partner, sometimes causing the introvert to feel crowded and the extravert to feel rejected.
- In conflict, the extraverted spouse's defenses tend toward aggression and the introvert's defenses tend toward withdrawal.
- Sometimes the introverted partner wants a deeper level of interaction than does the extravert.
- The extraverted spouse typically desires more social activity involving more people and expending more energy than does the introvert.

Analytical or Emotional Processing

- The analytical spouse can be perceived by the other as critical and uncaring, whereas the partner who processes more emotionally can be viewed by the other as overly dramatic or irrational.
- The spouse who processes emotionally focuses on feelings and needs, while the analytical partner focuses on diagnosing and solving problems.
- The analytical spouse makes decisions based more on logic, whereas the partner who processes emotionally bases decisions more on gut feelings.

Practical or Imaginative

- These partners sometimes lack enough common interests.
- The practical spouse is highly oriented to the concrete world and one's physical surroundings, while the imaginative partner can leave the concrete plane and become immersed in a world of creativity.
- The imaginative spouse needs variety and change, while the practical partner prefers order and routine.

"Take Charge" or "Go with the Flow"

- "Take Charge" can perceive "Go with the Flow" as being lazy and irresponsible, whereas "Go with the Flow" can view "Take Charge" as being too controlling.

- "Go with the Flow" and "Take Charge" are often at odds due to their differing priorities.

- "Take Charge" usually stresses "get it done" first and relax and play later, while "Go with the Flow" tends to relax and play now and "get it done" later.

By the time many couples come to therapy, partners have long been stuck in the power struggle of trying to change the other's personality. When they come to sit across from me, the message, "I can't accept you the way you are," has often been established and is difficult to repair. I hear statements like, "He was so much more attentive and affectionate when we were dating." The courtship stage of a relationship is often deceiving. In courtship, we work our hardest to connect. We are performing to some extent. Courtship behavior is usually not a totally accurate reflection of our personality. Some of our traits will likely be concealed during this stage. A couple who rushes from courtship to binding commitment is rolling the dice. It takes time to really get to know a person. In my observation, compatibility between the partners' personalities increases the odds for a successful marriage. Opposite personalities are more challenged to create harmony over the long haul.

Our personalities encompass a set of abilities and limitations and are the foundation of who we are. We may be able to tweak traits some, but they never change dramatically. Our personalities will express certain abilities intuitively, while other abilities will never come naturally to us. Nevertheless, a successful marriage requires us to express the full range of traits to some degree. The traits that don't come naturally will have to be practiced consciously. There are too many aspects of marriage that require conscious skills. The limitations of our personality don't let us off the hook for doing what it takes to succeed. Here are common examples of what personality types have to practice consciously at times to make their marriage work:

Extraverts:

- Give your partner space.
- Talk less and listen more.
- Pace yourself.
- Be more patient.
- Reflect more.

Introverts:

- Talk and engage more.
- Go out more.
- Be more assertive.
- Take more initiative.
- Take more risks.

Analytical:

- Orient more to how others feel and what they need.
- Express more warmth, empathy, and love.
- Listen more and fix less.
- Allow for more gray and less black and white.
- Let go of needing to be right
- Accept more and judge less.

Emotional:

- Distinguish more between feelings and reality to keep perspective.
- Maintain healthy boundaries.
- Avoid people-pleasing and care-taking patterns.
- Be more oriented to your own needs.
- Limit the drama.
- Be more assertive.

Practical:

- Take more risks.
- Add variety and spice to life
- Be more spontaneous.
- Use your imagination more.
- Be more flexible and tolerant.

Imaginative:

- Pay more attention to details.
- Establish more order.
- Stay in touch with the concrete world.
- Avoid reading people's minds.
- Keep the dark side of your imagination in check.

Take Charge:

- Control less and let go more.
- Be more spontaneous.
- Play more.
- Assume less sense of responsibility for others.
- Be more flexible and tolerant.

Go with the Flow:

- Assume more sense of responsibility for necessary tasks.
- Participate more in planning and decision-making.
- Be on time more.
- Procrastinate less.
- Establish more order.

When we have insight about personality, we can avoid misinterpreting behavior explained by our wiring. On the other hand, this insight informs us as to what we must practice consciously in order to succeed. Ideally, we come to value our differences and see them, instead, as complements and counter-balances to one another. Ultimately, we can learn from each other and become more whole.

Emotions: Behavior is often an expression of valid feelings.

You know you're the adult in the room once you've found yourself on the receiving end of your spouse's anger and can manage a non-defensive reaction. Imagine this scenario:

Karen has had a stressful day at work and has to rush to pick up her two children – one from daycare and the other from after-school care – in order to get home in time to begin the nightly routine, which requires Ron to be home in time to manage the kids while she prepares dinner. On this day, Ron has been delayed at work due to a stressful encounter with his boss; he's so preoccupied with the conflict, he neglects to let Karen know he's running behind schedule. By the time he gets home, Karen is fuming and meets him at the door on the attack. "Why are you so late? Where have you been and what have you been doing? Why didn't you call. Don't you care how I feel?"

Ron has a split second to override his instinct to defend himself. Every cell in his body wants to counter her attack, but if he does, her frustration will only escalate. If he can stop from reacting long enough to orient himself to the emotional energy that's controlling Karen, he will have achieved a rare level of consciousness that will likely produce a positive outcome. The key to this ability is insight about how emotional energy explains behavior.

What I've learned in the relatively few arguments over the course of my marriage was when Catherine expresses her anger, she's not an enemy attacking me. My defenses are inclined to hear her telling me I'm a bad person and a bad husband, which could set me off defensively. In reality, she isn't condemning me but, rather, feeling hurt or disrespected by something I've done or said. I've learned that when that kind of emotional energy presents itself to slow my reaction down and to observe and listen, rather than view her anger as a threat to defend against. I try to practice in those moments telling myself that the way I love her is to allow her to express her feelings and to try to understand her.

The more you fight something, the more you energize and empower it. In marriage, the more you defend against a spouse with intense feelings, the more you fuel those feelings. The adult knows that no one wins a fight; there are only losers. The mature solution is to disarm, avoid reacting to the behavior, and listen to the feelings. In many cases, the main need of the offended spouse is to feel heard, understood, and validated. Many problems are resolved simply by mature listening. Ironically, when partners can convert negative behavior into a conversation about vulnerable feelings that are met with empathy and respect, they are drawn closer.

Remember my examples of my taking shots at Catherine about clutter or the credit card bill? When I got to the heart of it, I was able to explain to her that clutter triggered stress and that confusing purchases triggered fears. It made all the difference when I was able to explain accurately my deeper feelings rather than express them defensively. When I experience Catherine's understanding and responsiveness to my stress and fears, I feel more loved by her and more love for her.

The insight of connecting behavior to feelings in order to redirect the dialogue to its most important level is critical to the success of a marriage. So, the next time you're on the receiving end of intense emotional behavior from your spouse, practice the following steps:

- Stop: Don't react and don't defend yourself.
- Wait: Observe, listen, and recover your ability to think rationally.
- Think: Remind yourself that your spouse's behavior is defensive and not intended to be malicious.
- Ask yourself what vulnerable feelings may be driving your spouse's behavior.

- Remind yourself that your best and loving response is to allow your partner to get the emotional energy out.
- Encourage your partner to identify the vulnerable feelings.
- Listen. Understand. Validate.

The next time your spouse does or says something that adversely affects you, before you react, stop and tell yourself, "This probably makes sense." Then ask, "What might explain this?" Quickly review the list of possibilities: an unmet need, learning, a personality trait, a vulnerable feeling. Then approach with an open mind and the intention to listen and understand. If you practice these steps, you will be the adult in the room.

Assertiveness Applied to Marriage

I assert myself skillfully in order to make myself understood and to get my needs met in my marriage.

If you're looking to measure the maturity in your marriage, gauge the extent skillful assertiveness is practiced. Why this skill is such a good indicator of maturity is explained by what true assertiveness reflects.

Why is it so difficult for spouses to talk rationally and respectfully about how they feel, why they feel the way they do, and what they want and need from each other? It may be because many people don't fully trust and validate themselves. Many can't identify what they really think or feel on a deep level and why, and consequently, don't know what they really need. In many cases, they only know when they're angry. I've come to respect how complex a skill true assertiveness is. To practice assertiveness, one must integrate other key adult traits: positive sense of self, independent thinking, personal responsibility, conscious thinking and feeling, and insight. If you know what to listen for, you'll hear these elements expressed in skillful assertiveness.

For years, Jane tolerated her husband Clayton's judgmental and sarcastic jabs at some of her personality traits. Naturally, his ridicule stung; yet, she never had a rational conversation with him about the effect of his comments or what she needed. She, on occasion, expressed anger defensively, but to no avail. Jane's resentment grew into a barrier to their closeness.

As I got to know Jane, I learned she unconsciously felt inferior to Clayton. He was more educated than she was and ran his own business; she was without a vocational niche. They had contrasting personalities. Jane was spontaneous, playful, and imaginative with highly creative interests. Conversely, Clayton was analytical and practical. He mocked her traits that he didn't understand or frustrated him. Jane unconsciously gave her husband's view of her credibility and tolerated his disrespect. During our work together, she gained a stronger sense of who she was and the validity of her own unique personality, thus empowering her to see herself as his equal and his ridicule as unacceptable. This stronger sense of self gave her the resolve, for the first time, to assert herself.

Jane requested time to talk with her husband about this very important obstacle in their relationship. Here is the essence of what she said to him:

> I'm long overdue in expressing some feelings I've had for a while. I've felt hurt, disrespected, and resentful because of the occasional sarcastic and judgmental comments you make about my personality. I really don't think you intend to hurt me, but it makes me feel like you don't fully respect and accept me for who I am. This has become a barrier to my feeling close to you. I want to feel closer, but I need to first believe I'm respected and accepted by you. I'm asking you to be more aware and sensitive about what you say and how you say it. I'm also asking you to be more affirming of me. I want us to be more conscious of how we relate to each other and to take the responsibility for addressing issues in a mature way before they go too far. I take responsibility for tolerating your comments and not explaining earlier how I felt and what I needed.

Jane's inability to validate her self-worth inhibited her from asserting herself in a truly empowered way. Once Clayton witnessed Jane's growing self-confidence and ability to be direct, he began to see her in a new light and with renewed respect. He also felt a new kind of accountability to her. This shift transformed their relationship.

To be clear, assertiveness is not the same as aggression or defensiveness, but rather a proactive expression of peacefully, but firmly, standing our own ground. Assertiveness is the act of communicating in a rational and respectful tone what we think and feel, what we want others to understand or consider, and in some cases, what we want or need from others. Assertiveness can be as nuanced as expressing an opinion or preference, or as simple as making a request. Assertiveness enables healthy boundaries and allows us to say no when needed. Sometimes it means explaining our rationale for decisions. Skilled assertiveness is essential to the successful resolution of conflict. Don't expect to get your needs met in a marriage without it. I'm convinced many more marriages would survive, if not thrive, if skilled assertiveness was common practice.

Ann and Steve had a pattern in which planning vacations turned into arguments complete with a winner and a loser. To Ann, vacations were an opportunity to indulge themselves; she would push for trips that could stretch their budget. However, all Steve could see were dollar signs which only stressed and prevented him from enjoying the trip. Because Ann tended towards the aggressive and Steve toward the passive, Ann tended to be the victor of these battles, leaving Steve, the loser, stressed about money and resentful. Steve never rationally explained to Ann his deeper fears and anxiety that may have given her insight and empathy in discussions about vacations. One of the barriers in their dynamic was Steve's life-long pattern of people-pleasing, a reflection of his powerful fears of outside disapproval and a lack of orientation to the validity of his own needs. Once he reached a point in therapy in which he could validate more of what he thought, felt, wanted, and needed, he was prepared to be assertive with Ann. With some coaching, this is what he was able to express to her.

> There is something I need to explain to you and it would really help me if you could understand. Our conflict about vacation decisions has caused me real distress and some anger toward you that I want to resolve. I accept responsibility for my own defensive reactions and not expressing myself well, and I want to correct that now. I also know that those arguments are distressing to you.
>
> I think we each have valid but conflicting needs when it comes to our vacations. I understand you want our vacations to be a unique and special experience, and I respect and want that too, but sometimes I bear the weight of our finances. If I feel our vacation is beyond our means, not only can I not enjoy the trip, but the vacation adds to the stress that the time off is intended to relieve me from. The next time we approach the vacation discussion, I would like for us to start with an awareness of what we each want and need that will make our vacation enjoyable for both of us. Hopefully, we can be creative and come up with ideas that make it a treat for you and feel affordable to me.

Marriage is an on-going negotiation between two people whose thoughts, feelings, wants and needs occasionally and inevitably conflict. In a childish marriage, conflict is a power struggle with a short term winner and loser, and only losers in the long term. In an adult marriage, the partners are committed to resolving conflicts with a win-win. In a childish marriage, the words, "We need to talk," usually mean someone is going to get a tongue-lashing. In an adult marriage, "We need to talk," is a good sign for several reasons. First, there is trust that what needs to be addressed will be presented skillfully, with love and respect, and will involve listening. Secondly, there is agreement that the relationship is far more secure when issues are addressed proactively rather than allowed to simmer under the surface until they erupt. "We need to talk" is viewed as positive also because it is evidence of one's investment in keeping the relationship on the right track by taking personal responsibility for making oneself better understood. Finally, in an adult marriage, "We need to talk" leads to the positive outcome of deeper understanding and closeness, thanks to the tone and the skill used.

I've grown weary over the years of hearing some partners tell me that they shouldn't have to spell out to their spouses how they feel and what they want or need. Some believe that love is magic and that, if we really love each other, we will intuit each other's feelings and needs. Then, when their spouses have not read their minds and fail to respond to silent expectations, they become deeply hurt and angry because they perceive their partners don't care enough. In reality, spouses can be in the same room and be on different planets by virtue of their differences in wiring. Women tend to be more intuitive about feelings and needs, and men tend to be less attuned to the emotional climate. The sooner we accept that love doesn't determine intuitiveness and let go of that brand of magical thinking, the better marriages will work.

We'd only just sat down for a recent counseling session when Dawn launched into a litany of complaints about things Mel was doing wrong. The emotional intensity from Dawn expressed a backlog of hurt, anger, and mistrust of Mel's intentions. I've learned to listen for underlying themes in people's complaints so I can steer the conversation to the heart of the matter.

This couple's lives were stressful. They had three young children, and both Dawn and Mel had demanding jobs. I deciphered her protests to mean she felt disconnected from Mel and believed he was not making time with her a priority, shorthand for he didn't love her enough. While looking through this perceptual lens,

Dawn built a case against Mel by collecting every bit of evidence she could find to confirm her view. We can all be quite adept at twisting and turning details to confirm our perceptions. From prior work with this couple, my sense was Mel truly loved Dawn and was, in fact, devoted to her.

When I asked Dawn to dig deeper into her grievances to identify the vulnerable feelings and her needs, she fell silent. She didn't know how to answer those questions. She then told me she shouldn't have to spell out what she needed and that if Mel cared enough, those answers would be obvious to him. She literally expected him to read her mind, and every failure to do so was evidence of a lack of commitment.

I explained to Dawn that an adult marriage requires partners to spell out, proactively, feelings of being disconnected, unloved, and hurt. If she wondered where she stood on his list of priorities, it was her responsibility to raise the question. I added that she also is required to explain that she needs to feel closer to and more loved by him. I then asked Dawn to make a specific request or two that would help meet her need. Dawn thought for a moment and then requested that after they put the kids to bed, they sit together with the T.V. off, have a glass of wine, and talk about things other than work for no more than thirty minutes. With a puzzled look, Mel asked, "That's all it takes? Why didn't you ask for that earlier?" To which Dawn replied, "Because I shouldn't have to." We still had some work to do, but that was progress. This is also an example of how a distorted expectation of how a marriage should work was causing needless pain.

Yes, in an adult marriage you have to spell out what you want understood. Here are some key elements that are part of effective assertiveness:

- Develop consciousness of what you think, feel, want, and need and a belief in its validity.

- Look for times and opportunities to express yourself proactively, rationally, and respectfully with sensitivity to your spouse's thoughts, feelings, wants, and needs in order to prevent misunderstanding and conflict.
- Never lose sight of the fact that you're married to a flawed, limited human being who at times is not aware of your feelings and needs, so give him or her the benefit of the doubt.
- When negative feelings signal misunderstanding and conflict, first ask yourself these questions:

> What are my specific feelings, particularly vulnerable ones, and what are they really about?
>
> Is this about small stuff or big stuff?
>
> What is my perception and could it be distorted? What am I telling myself?
>
> Might there be an explanation for this that I don't see?
>
> What are my expectations and are they realistic?
>
> Am I doing something to contribute to the problem that I need to take some responsibility for?

- Make a conscious decision to address the issue assertively.
- Organize your thoughts and feelings, and rehearse what to say and how to say it rationally and respectfully.
- Request a time to talk that is good for both of you.
- Introduce the conversation with defense lowering techniques. Examples:

> "I'm bringing this up to prevent negative
> feelings from getting in the way of our
> closeness."

> "I know you have valid complaints about
> me at times that I want you to be able to
> bring up."

- Preface statements with language such as "It seems to me" and "My perception is." Avoid accusatory language.
- Explain how you feel and why.
- Acknowledge any responsibility you share for the problem.
- Try to balance the negatives with some positives, if possible.
- Ask for what you want. Make specific, concrete requests that will help meet your need.
- Listen respectfully to your partner's point of view, and look for opportunities to validate his or her thoughts and feelings. Avoid needing to be right and win a debate. Be open to a new perception.
- Seek a win-win understanding for the future.

Back to Dawn, who expected Mel to read her mind and believed she shouldn't have to spell out her feelings and needs to him. Here is the statement I wanted her to express by incorporating some of the above elements of assertiveness:

> I need to tell you that lately I've been feeling
> somewhat hurt and even a little unloved by you. It
> seems our lives are so consumed with work and
> kids and T.V. that we're getting disconnected, and
> sometimes I wonder how much of a priority our
> relationship is to you. I know you're devoted to
> the kids and to your work, and I do trust that you
> love me, but right now I need a little more

evidence. I share some responsibility for our relationship getting lost in the shuffle. I could take more initiative and be more assertive. Sometimes I expect you to read my mind and that's not fair to you. One thing I'd like to ask for, that would help me feel closer to you day to day, is after we put the kids to bed, we turn off the television, pour a glass of wine, and talk about anything other than work for at least thirty minutes and, if we're on a roll, no more than an hour. I want both of us to feel responsible for taking care of our relationship and keeping ourselves close. Just as I'm doing now, I want you to feel free to bring up issues you have with me as well, so that we don't let hard feelings build up.

Take a few minutes to reflect on whether or not there is an issue or a pattern in your marriage that is causing a buildup of negative feelings. If so, you have a responsibility, as an adult, to address the problem assertively by following the steps outlined in this section. As you go forward in your marriage, look for opportunities to establish, as common practice, assertive communication to enhance your relationship and prevent problems. Review the assertiveness section in the first part of this book, and apply those recommended skills to your marriage. Skillful assertiveness is fundamental to a mature marriage. I often say to couples that in a mature marriage, "no news is good news" because each partner is secure in the trust of knowing that if the other has a significant complaint, some building negative feelings, an unmet need, or anything important that needs to be expressed, the issue will be addressed early and assertively. In an adult marriage, when there are no complaints, all is well.

Sacrifice Applied to Marriage

I balance making sacrifices for the needs of my spouse and tending to my own valid needs.

My work with couples aims to help partners consciously embrace the commitment to make sacrifices for each other as an investment in their future happiness. Here are a few examples from my couple work in which sacrifice was the issue.

- Bob and Teresa had each been previously married and had lived in different cities. After they married, Teresa moved into Bob's home where he had lived for years with his first wife. Many of their shared home's decorations and furnishings remained from Bob's first marriage. By taking up residency in Bob's city and home, Teresa moved into Bob's world. Needless to say, she soon began to feel uncomfortable surrounded by so many trappings of his past life along with the sense that she was living in his house and not theirs. Bob, on the other hand, was quite content with this arrangement and reacted defensively when Teresa began to express discomfort. When she wanted to make changes in the house, he resisted. Bob needed to come to the realization that if he wanted his marriage to work, he needed to do whatever it would take to help Teresa feel it was as much her home as it was his, even if that meant considering relocation altogether.

- Derek and Melissa had been married for ten years and had two young children. Their timeline together was

landmarked by several cross-country moves due to
Derek's job promotions. Fulfilling his career ambitions
was a high priority for Derek, but this lifestyle prevented
them from establishing roots while also limiting Melissa's
ability to accomplish some of her own goals. Once Derek
was finally able to remain in a location long enough for
them to build friendships and invest in their community,
Melissa was able to land the educational consulting
contract work that she hoped for. When Derek got the
next promotion opportunity that required another move,
Melissa's patience was spent and she instead advocated for
herself and the kids. As much as Derek wanted to advance
within his company, it was time for him to make Melissa's
needs the priority.

- Scott and Sharon had been married for eighteen years and
  had two teenagers. Scott was a successful real estate
  broker, which provided an affluent lifestyle for his family.
  Sharon worked as a school teacher the first few years of
  their marriage, but left to take on the job of full-time
  mom. When the recession hit, Scott's business was
  devastated, and likewise, their family's income took a
  nosedive. Scott quickly became overwhelmed with the
  burden to maintain their standard of living. Scott
  recognized they either had to make drastic changes in their
  lifestyle, or Sharon had to return to work. At first, Sharon
  was in denial about the seriousness of their situation and
  was resistant to make the necessary sacrifices. Once she
  realized her true priority and conviction of "we're in this
  together," she began to share the sense of responsibility
  for their family's financial picture. She ultimately did make
  major lifestyle changes and re-entered the job market.
  Even though the changes were stressful, they enhanced
  Scott's and Sharon's closeness thanks to their renewed
  sense of partnership.

Most of us enter marriage with a sense of adventure, stars in our eyes, and peaking sex drives, but once settled in, we encounter the collision of our differences and needs. In the early stages of marriage, it's easy to be disillusioned and threatened by conflict. We tend to react to the discord instinctively, engage in power struggles, and are at risk to get lost in our defenses. We don't realize we are acting out a timeless drama – a process with predictable stages and a learning curve. Hopefully, we have enough maturity going in to the marriage to navigate the early stages while we're learning the lessons that marriage has to teach us.

As I explained in the first section of this book, I encountered this learning curve in my own life. Marriage was trying to teach me that if I was going to succeed, I would have to choose to "sign up" and willingly make sacrifices for the needs of a partner. It was a gradual process, but when I eventually resolved my resistance, living in our marriage became easier and more satisfying. The curriculum at the heart of this process is learning to value and to prioritize your partners' needs as much as you do your own.

The unwillingness to sacrifice can destroy a marriage. More often than not, men tend to be the biggest offenders of this marital issue. Here are a few of the more extreme examples I have encountered:

- Two wives have told me they delivered a child while their husband was on the golf course.
- Several wives have reported being ill and bedridden while their husbands did little, if anything, to attend to them or pick up the slack around the house.
- Many wives have described being solely responsible for their young children while their husbands watched T.V., played video games, or were lost in cyber-space.
- Too many husbands justify being gone every Saturday or Sunday to play golf or fish while the needs of home and family go neglected.

- There are husbands who stop by their favorite watering hole each day after work and arrive home late.
- Some husbands never follow through on promises to handle vital home repairs and maintenance directly impacting their wives.

These spouses embody the epitome of children in grown-up bodies. I hesitate to use these more extreme examples because they may make some partners, who don't deserve it, look good by comparison. But these examples reflect how unprepared some people can be for the level of sacrifice required of a successful marriage.

Most of us entering marriage are mature enough to understand and accept we have to make sacrifices to make marriage work. However, few of us are prepared for how dramatically we have to re-orient ourselves from "me" to "we" and how constantly we are tested on this issue. Every day we have to willingly sacrifice some of our freedom, time, money, energy, sleep, play, lifestyle, and other individual priorities. Those who enter marriage with a dominant "me" orientation will likely have to overcome resistance to these daily tests, while those entering marriage with a head-start on the "we" orientation will resolve the sacrifice challenge with more ease.

One morning recently, Catherine told me she had a miserable and sleepless night. It was one of those nights when you can't sleep for worrying about everything under the sun. My wife is not typically a worrier. She was slightly tormented as she lay tossing and turning with her obsessive thoughts. Catherine told me she had considered waking me to reassure her everything would be OK, but decided not to bother me and guessed I'd be irritated by such a wake-up. I admit there probably was a time when being awakened may have bothered me, but I believe I've long since outgrown that kind of selfishness. In fact, I found myself slightly hurt that she thought I wouldn't want her to wake me for help of any kind. The difference between me then and now is that, at an earlier time in our marriage, had she awakened me, I would have offered her reassurance while thinking, "I hope I can get back to sleep." Now, I would be thinking, "I'm glad I can be here for her," and "I'm grateful we can be here for each other." That's the difference between "me" and "we".

Although marriage, at times, can demand dramatic sacrifice, more often sacrifice is found in the subtle ways we are asked to leave our comfort zone. Consider Bill and Susan who were in their mid-thirties with a two-year old son. While Susan, an extravert, had always enjoyed her work, the couple agreed she would stay home to care for their son. When Susan was employed, more engaged in the outside world, and they were freer to get out more together, she felt close to Bill. As life as a stay-at-home mom unfolded, Susan began to feel the effects of social isolation; she particularly missed adult conversation which exposed a weakness in the quality of hers and Bill's interaction. Meanwhile, Bill's introversion inclined him to come home from work and withdraw in front of the television to recharge his battery. When Susan attempted to talk with Bill, he would respond minimally, not really engaging. Bill loved Susan, but was unconsciously allowing his personality to make him unavailable to her. As time went on, Susan felt increasingly disconnected from Bill.

Two things had to happen. First, Susan had to assert herself by explaining to Bill how she felt and what she needed from him. Up to that point, she had expressed her feelings only defensively. Secondly, Bill had to choose, consciously, to leave his comfort zone when he came home from work. He had to understand that Susan had a valid need and was making a valid request of him to engage more with her in the evening. Bill's introversion was not an acceptable excuse for neglecting to interact with Susan. Bill was simply going to have to choose to practice skills and habits that did not come naturally to him. There are countless ways in a marriage we must consciously practice reaching outside our comfort zones to make the relationship work.

One of our deepest needs in marriage is to feel a sense of partnership – to feel the security of knowing that we are in this together, that we help each other get through the day, share the workload, comfort and console, affirm and encourage each other. The orientation to "we" is expressed in the small things that form a critical mass. Here are a few examples:

- Keeping your spouse informed about your whereabouts and plans such as having to work late, running late, or upcoming travel
- Consulting your spouse before making decisions, commitments, or purchases that have a direct impact on him or her
- Asking your spouse if he or she needs anything while you are out running errands or shopping
- Asking your spouse what you can do to help when he or she seems frazzled
- Making a priority of spending time together
- Advocating for your spouse in relation to your family, if needed
- Accompanying your spouse to an activity or gathering that you would not otherwise choose, in order to be supportive
- Making sure that you're doing your share of the work related to the house and the kids
- Practicing awareness and sensitivity to your spouse's feelings and needs and responding positively to your spouse's need-related requests
- Willingly making reasonable compromises to resolve conflicts
- Initiating efforts to enhance closeness with your spouse
- Saying "please" and "thank you" often

- Looking for opportunities to compliment and affirm your spouse
- Expressing simple loving gestures regularly
- Really listening

A marriage consists of three entities – two individuals and a relationship. The relationship is, in a sense, like a child in need of nurturing for which both partners are equally responsible. Anyone with children knows how much sacrifice is required to care for the needs of a child. A mature orientation to the needs of a marriage relationship is similar. If you're married, review the previous list with your partner to assess how consciously both of you are taking care of your relationship. Use the list as a springboard for targeting needs, making requests, and making your own additions to the list that enhance the "we" orientation.

Sacrifice in marriage is also about accountability to a partner. Sometimes marital problems are caused by one spouse's mental health issues such as

- Attention deficit disorder
- Obsessive compulsive disorder
- A chronic mood disorder such as anxiety or depression
- Bi-polar disorder
- An eating disorder
- Some type of addiction
- Compulsive spending
- Sexual dysfunction
- Obesity

Obviously, these issues can be a source of great stress to a marriage. I've worked with many marriages in which one spouse exhibited marked symptoms of one or more of these problems, but wasn't taking responsibility for addressing them. Not only is this about personal responsibility, but it's also about sacrifice because of the serious commitment required to deal with mental health issues for the good of the marriage. It's asking too much of your spouse to absorb the consequences of these problems, particularly if they are unaddressed. If you intend to have a mature marriage, you're accountable to your spouse for taking care of your own physical and mental health.

In an adult marriage, both partners feel the sacrifices are mutual and balanced and are conscious of their respective sacrifices, but without keeping score. In such a marriage, sacrifices feel like good investments in a blue chip stock that is growing and paying solid dividends for the benefit of both, but without strings attached. In a childish marriage, either no one is making enough sacrifice for the other and it is "every man for himself," dictated by a "me" orientation, or one person is doing too much of the work based on his or her fear, insecurity, dependence, and caretaking.

If you are in the latter version of a marriage and there is little to no return on your investment, then something needs to give. If your marriage is a source of chronic stress or depression, something needs to give. You're doing yourself damage, which is in no way virtuous or adult. Along the way, you may have become lost and disconnected from who you are and what you need. You should expect your marriage to enhance the quality of your life. If you intend to be an adult, it is your responsibility to take care of yourself and see to it that there is balance in the level of sacrifice in your marriage. The previous section on assertiveness should have given you key tools with which to address any imbalance in sacrifice.

If your marriage has reached a point in which you feel that your physical, mental, or emotional health is being sacrificed due to your partner's abuse, neglect, addictions, recklessness, or irresponsibility, you have wandered way off track. In this case, the only healthy and adult options are to require dramatic changes or prepare to leave. Choosing to stay in a destructive marriage is symptomatic of being a child in a grown-up body.

As you might imagine, the process of writing this book has required me to reflect on my own maturity level related to each adult trait. Writing about sacrifice in marriage has made me acutely aware of how much Catherine sacrifices for me. Although I make sacrifices for her, this writing has reminded me I still have work to do. I hope these words inspire you as well to assess your level of sacrifice in your marriage. If you and your spouse agree that the level of sacrifice feels balanced, then congratulations are in order. Keep up the good work! If you are concluding that you're either sacrificing too much or too little, then something needs to change. I hope I've motivated you to take the next step toward being the adult in the room.

Competence Applied to Marriage

I stated at the beginning of this section on "The Adult in Marriage" that I do not address separately the trait of competence applied to marriage. When you apply the other adult traits to marriage, the result is, in effect, marital competence. I hope you've recognized and taken to heart the many insights and skills embedded in this entire section. Any attempt to further distinguish marital competence from what I've covered to this point would only be redundant. So let's move on to the next trait.

Personal Growth Applied to Marriage

I am committed to my ongoing learning and growth and to taking emotional risks in my marriage.

Greg and Diane came to counseling, like many couples who come through my door, mired in layers of unconscious patterns that were damaging their marriage. They embodied contrasting personalities and were driven by unconscious programs: Greg was a people-pleaser, and Diane was a classic caretaker. They grew up in very different family cultures. They also had the stresses of parenting four young children. Diane's "caretaker" programming gave her a sense of responsibility for all the outcomes, the cause of much fear and stress. In fact, Diane seemed to look for things to worry about. Her anxiety coupled with her high extraversion, expressed itself in reactivity, over-control, and criticism, particularly of Greg. Greg's "people-pleaser" programming, along with his marked introversion, inhibited him from setting healthy boundaries at work, engaging socially, and asserting himself, particularly with his parents and Diane. In addition, Greg's quietness, at times, troubled Diane, giving her one more thing to worry about. Diane was convinced something was wrong with Greg and it was up to her to fix it. Their interaction was marked by her nagging him and him placating her, while both repressed resentments.

The good news was they still loved each other and were committed to the success of their marriage. They both freely acknowledged responsibility for contributing to their negative dynamic and were receptive to learning the insights and skills required of them to solve their problems.

There was much dissecting to be done. We had to pull back the curtain on their relationship to reveal the programs and patterns in which they were lost. I asked them to complete a personality assessment to help illustrate and validate their differences, particularly his introversion and her extraversion. This process explained objectively much of their misunderstanding and distorted perceptions of one another. Framing for them how Diane's caretaking and Greg's people-pleasing were at the root of many of their problems was both revelatory and empowering for them. Diane began to consciously practice accepting and trusting Greg more. She also had to get a handle on her reactivity and express herself more constructively. Another challenge for Diane was to let go of the responsibility she felt for everything. Greg had to learn to validate and assert himself at work, with his parents, and with Diane. He also had to make a conscious effort to interact with Diane more.

Greg and Diane's commitment and efforts began to pay off almost immediately. As they continued practicing the new insights and skills, their relationship improved dramatically. Greg and Diane are just another of countless examples I could cite of how a couple's commitment to learning and growth made them the adults in the room and all the difference in their marriage.

Somewhere along the way, I either read or was told what has turned out to be my favorite description of marriage. Yet, I'm embarrassed to admit I can't remember where this nugget came from; otherwise, I would gladly credit its author. Nevertheless, this description deserves to be shared because it is both simple and profound. Here it is: "Marriage is the process of learning how to love."

Marriage is a laboratory and your spouse is your lab partner. The lab work involves ongoing experimentation, and every few weeks you're tested with new problems to solve. If we viewed marriage less as a ticket to love and more as a curriculum for love, we would be more intentional about learning its lessons and thus more oriented for success. Conceptualizing marriage as curriculum requires us to first admit we have much to learn about how to love deeply and maturely. So, in effect, marriage is a kind of higher education to which we must commit ourselves. Another way to think about this educational process is to imagine that you and your partner speak different languages. It is incumbent on each of you not only to learn and to practice your partner's language, but to teach your partner your language as well. Imagine how conscious and careful you would have to be to communicate effectively.

In fact, I often recommend to couples a book entitled *The Five Love Languages* by Gary Chapman. Chapman introduces the idea that each of us has a dominant style of communicating love. He has identified five categories that capture these different forms in which love is both expressed and perceived. With this insight, couples can become more conscious of expressing love in the form that speaks to the other. They can also better recognize love expressed toward them in forms different from their own. For example, one spouse may express love through gift giving, whereas the other feels most loved when they spend quality time together. Another partner may express love through acts of service, whereas the other feels most loved by words of affirmation. Consciously applying love languages is a tangible expression of one's commitment to learning how to love.

When we're truly receptive to learning how to love in marriage, we are less defensive and more open to our partner's feedback. We protect ourselves less and risk being vulnerable more by admitting our weaknesses, fears, hurts, and insecurities. Ironically, we are the safest in a marriage when we're not defending or protecting ourselves. Making ourselves vulnerable is what creates closeness.

The marriage relationship has been evolving from the beginning of time, but I think it's safe to say, in the context of history, the marriage dynamic has changed most dramatically within the last fifty years in the United States. There's no doubt the women's movement in this country has shaken the traditional marriage paradigm of the early twentieth century. As women gained more access, opportunities, choices, and independence, they became less dependent on a husband and more empowered to require a higher set of expectations of marriage – the right kind of expectations. For example, the expectation of intimacy is a relatively new addition to our collective vision of marriage. This new concept of intimacy is more about closeness than sex. I doubt if my grandparents could imagine the equal partnerships that define many marriages today.

In the short term, these higher expectations have been disruptive and have sped the divorce rate, but as we slowly and gradually learn to create more equal and loving partnerships, everyone grows. Women have grown a stronger sense of self with more independence and assertiveness. Men express more empathy, compassion, and sensitivity to needs. In effect, this new brand of marriage is transforming men and women in very positive ways. In just the two and a half decades that I've worked closely with marriages, I've observed these marked changes. Women deserve most of the credit for this transformation. When couples arrive for counseling, roughly ninety percent of the time it's the wife who is the driving force, determined to raise the quality of the relationship.

What I've addressed in this section on applying the traits of the adult to marriage accounts for much of the curriculum and the competencies required for making a marriage work. By now, you should have identified some learning and growth goals related to these traits as they apply to your relationship.

The idea of learning and growth sounds great to most people, but it can also seem so abstract we don't know where to start. Sometimes we find ourselves so far off track that the thought of righting the ship can seem overwhelming. In my experience, there is only one way we humans make changes – one day at a time and one incremental step at a time. But once we take those new steps, we have to practice them consistently so they become habits. Remember the ancient saying: "The journey of a thousand miles begins with the first step."

Apply the following list of steps to your marriage and you will consciously put yourself on the path to learning how to love. These steps are to be practiced one day at a time and one incremental step at a time. Once started, they must be repeated over and over.

- Acknowledge you're a flawed, imperfect person who has much to learn about how to love.

- Make a conscious decision to be a more loving partner.

- Envision yourself as a more loving partner.

- Step back and practice observing the dynamics of your relationship.

- Read Gary Chapman's *The Five Love Languages.*

- Ask your partner to identify a few specific and concrete actions you can then practice to communicate love.

- Practice being more conscious of your own thoughts, feelings, and perceptions in relation to your partner.

- Practice being more conscious and intentional about your responses to your partner.

- Ask your partner to give you constructive feedback regarding something you do that causes frustration, hurt, fear, anger, confusion, stress, etc., and to make a constructive request of you.

- Acknowledge responsibility for a mistake or an insensitivity and make amends.

- Focus on your partner's strengths and what you love and respect and affirm those strengths.

- Focus on what your partner does for you and express gratitude.

- Tell your partner about your day's experience.

- Tell your partner about your deeper thoughts and feelings.

- Really listen when your partner is talking to you.

- Ask your partner if there is something you can help with.

- Suggest doing something enjoyable together.

- Express affection.

- Practice patience and acceptance with the "small stuff."

- Practice assertiveness with the "big stuff."

- Add to this list.

Each step on this list is very doable on most days. If you repeat these steps over and over, the journey of a thousand miles will begin to feel like the deeply satisfying adventure of a lifetime marriage has the potential to be. In a mature marriage, partners understand that, no matter the dynamic, they are both responsible for its creation. The partners who are quick to own their responsibility when there are problems and who readily seek to learn how to correct them are truly the adults in the room.

Three: The Adult as a Parent

"The task of rearing and guiding children can best be represented by the metaphor of raising plants. This should be encouraging, because raising plants is one of mankind's most successful activities. Perhaps the success comes from the fact that the gardener does not try to thrust impossible patterns on his plants. He respects their peculiarities, tries to provide suitable conditions, protects them from the more serious kinds of injury – but he lets the plant do the growing. He does not poke at the seed in order to make it sprout more quickly, nor does he seize the shoots when it breaks ground and try to pull open the first leaves by hand. Neither does he trim the leaves of different kinds of plants in order to have them all look alike. The attitude of the gardener is appropriate in dealing with children. It is the children who must do the growing, and they can do it only through the push of their own budding interests.

"The nurturing of growth requires the long patience of the gardener rather than the hasty intervention of the mechanic. It requires waiting for impulse to declare itself, for interest to appear, for initiative to come forth. It calls for a tolerant attitude toward individuality, respect for the unique pattern that unfolds in every case. It demands confidence that, in the long run, individuality will be an asset, not a handicap, and that it will lead both to a happier life and to a better world than if the goal had been set at conformity, pleasantness, marketability, or a pattern that is merely the empty logical opposite of mental and emotional disorder."

~ Robert White
Lives in Progress

Personal Responsibility Applied to Parenting

I accept responsibility for meeting the needs of my child.

If it were not for the damage done by the parenting of children in grown-up bodies, we therapists would not be in business. Truly, there is no greater responsibility than that of a parent. I was mistaken earlier when I said that marriage most reveals our level of maturity. In truth, the case for parenting is just as strong!

This section will highlight the differences between mature and immature parenting. Don't presume this to be a comprehensive parenting manual; there is simply too much ground to cover, and for that reason, I recommend parents devote themselves to some formal study regarding child development and effective parenting. There are too many crucial insights and strategies necessary to good parenting that don't come to us instinctively, but it is the adult in the room who makes the extra effort to develop these competencies.

In this section on parenting, I apply the traits of the adult on two levels: the first addresses how each trait within the parent, or the lack thereof, influences the quality of parenting. The second level addresses how to plant the seeds of these traits in children. Just as I introduced the section on marriage with the trait of **personal responsibility**, so, too, will I begin this section on the adult in parenting.

There are two primary responsibilities that encompass parenting: nurturing and teaching. All of the various functions of parenting flow from these two roles. Successfully fulfilling these two

parenting responsibilities requires the conscious application of all
of the other adult traits.

Nurturing: I take responsibility for understanding and meeting the nurturing needs of my child.

Meeting the nurturing needs of your children demands that you
understand their physical, psychological, and emotional needs at
each stage of their development and practice the consciousness to
create for your child a need-satisfying environment within which
to grow. Obviously, this means you must be acutely oriented to
your child's needs and have the maturity to sublimate your own
needs at times in favor of your child. This, of course, is easier said
than done, even for the most mature among us. It's not always
easy after a long hard day of work, to give your child the attention
needed from you, but those who do it are the adults in the room.
Four of five of Gary Chapman's "Love Languages," in many
ways, capture what it takes to nurture:

- physical touch
- quality time
- acts of service
- words of affirmation

The essential difference between mature and immature parenting
is that adults understand consciously they are responsible for
meeting the needs of their children and equip themselves for the
job, whereas children in grown-up bodies are not only
unequipped, but unconsciously depend on their children to meet
their needs. I have heard too many clients who were parented by
children in grown-up bodies say, "As long as I can remember, no
matter what was going on, it was always about Mom or Dad. It
was rarely about what I needed."

Once again, this relates back to Maslow's hierarchy of needs. First
and foremost, children need to feel consistently physically and
psychologically safe and free from fear. They need to know they're
in strong hands and can rely on being taken care of, that they are

unconditionally loved and accepted for who they are and they need to experience a sense of belonging through bonding and closeness. Children need to feel affirmed and validated, to see evidence of their significance, and to be empowered through encouragement to do their own thinking and to make developmentally appropriate decisions. Gary Smalley's and John Trent's best-selling book, *The Blessing*, framed, beautifully, the powerful need we all have to receive our parents' blessing to be who we are – the net effect of having these needs satisfied.

Children's needs are best met when they experience nurturing from both parents. There are still fathers out there who are content to leave the nurturing role to mothers, as if a father's nurture is unnecessary. My unscientific observation is that "father issues" are at the top of the list of barriers in the lives of my clients, with "mother issues" a close second. It is heartening, however, to observe the progress fathers have made on the nurturing front compared to fifty years ago, but there is still work to be done.

It's never too late to give your child, even a grown child, "the blessing." I routinely work with people in their twenties, thirties, and forties whose childhood wounds would be helped to heal by redemptive messages from a parent. If you feel that your parenting fell short when your child was younger, never underestimate the power you still have to promote healing.

Here are a few real life scenarios described by clients whose nurturing needs were not met because their parents were likely children in grown-up bodies:

- Pam's parents divorced when she was two. Her father abandoned the family, and her co-dependent mother went on to have three more unsuccessful marriages with partners disinterested in Pam. Pam remembers vividly worrying about her mother's insecurities and bouts with depression. She felt responsible for making

her mother happy and tried endlessly to make her
mother proud and earn her approval. As an adult, Pam
struggles to validate her own needs.

- Luke's father was a functional alcoholic who drank
  each night after work, numbing himself in front of the
  T.V. until he either went to bed or fell asleep in his
  recliner. His father rarely engaged with Luke at home.
  Luke struggles with a lingering sense of insignificance.

- Chuck had undiagnosed ADHD as a child. He was in
  constant motion, impulsive, and highly distractible. He
  would have been a challenge for any parent, but his
  parents viewed him as lazy, irresponsible, and a
  troublemaker and they told him so often. Sadly, Chuck
  eventually believed them.

- Shelly grew up in a very stressful home where she and
  her siblings were on the receiving end of constant
  criticism. She's mistrustful, quick to perceive others as
  criticizing her, and often relates defensively to people.
  Consequently, she has few friends.

- Rhonda's mother was a perfectionist and expected
  Rhonda to be the best at everything, as well as look
  perfect. To Rhonda's mother, one's image and
  impressing people were the priorities. Rhonda never
  feels good enough and struggles with anorexia.

- Cameron is gay. He is twenty-four and afraid to tell his
  parents about his sexual orientation; they're adamant
  that homosexuality is both wrong and a personal
  choice. Cameron believes he would be fundamentally
  unacceptable in the eyes of his parents and struggles to
  accept himself.

- Helen grew up with a father who was chronically angry
  and prone to rages. When he was home, everyone

walked on eggshells. Today Helen is hypersensitive to disapproval and extremely afraid of anger and conflict.

I could go on citing examples like these, but you get the picture. Certainly, many people who use counseling did get their needs for nurture met, but those clients are the exceptions to the rule.

The adults in the room can tell you what they practice consciously and strategically day in and day out to be responsive to their child's needs. Children in grown-up bodies are so pre-occupied with their own un-met needs, insecurities, and stresses that they parent mostly in reaction to their child. In fact, often their child represents just another source of stress. These parents may unconsciously resent their child for having needs.

There are also the parents who are in such need of their child's love they become enmeshed with their child and smother them with obsessive attention. These parents rise and fall with the changing moods of their child.

Even though the best parents have their bad days and make plenty of mistakes, if you were a fly on the wall in the home of a mature parent, here is what you would generally observe related to nurturing:

- An overall sense of order with established routines and sense of comfort and calmness due to living proactively; the sense of safety and security is palpable.

- Mostly positive engagement between parent and child with interaction marked by a warm, rational, and respectful tone toward the child.

- Parents listening to the child with undivided attention and statements of validation and empathy in response to the child's thoughts and feelings.

- Frequent loving touches; hugs are routine.

- Parents generally seize on opportunities to spend time with their children and also plan for it. Examples: bathing the child, reading to the child, playing on the floor together, throwing the ball together, helping with homework, going on outings together, teaching the child how to do something, attending the child's school and community activities.

- Frequent affirming statements about both what the child does and who the child is as a person.

As a parent, your responsibility to nurture is profound. Make no mistake, the degree to which your children's nurturing needs are satisfied can set the stage for the rest of their lives. You don't have to be the perfect parent. You can be flawed and make mistakes, but if, overall, your parenting is characterized by these elements, your children's nurturing needs will likely be satisfied. Two excellent resources that serve as guides for meeting the nurturing needs of children are Gary Chapman and Ross Campbell's *Love Languages of Children* and Chapman's *The Five Love Languages of Teenagers.*

Teaching: I take responsibility for teaching my child how to live a healthy and independent life.

As a parent, you can't avoid teaching. The only question is: what are you teaching? Who you are, your values, how you live your life, what you do and say in the presence of your child, even your absence, all teach your child something. Immature parents are unconscious of this fact and thus teach their child how to live unconsciously. Adults are acutely aware of the power of their teaching and the various ways in which they teach. Their consciousness empowers them to teach strategically in order to empower their child.

We parents often make the mistake of expecting our children and teenagers to grasp insights and skills that actually can't be fully realized until their twenties, when they're brains have been fully developed. We also make the mistake of assuming our children know how to do things instinctively without needing to be taught.

As a young father of two little boys, I had to be awakened to how much teaching is involved in parenting. I remember one such wake-up call vividly. Our oldest son was seven and our youngest was four. We had a nightly routine that required them to take their baths, one right after the other. They'd both been taught to bathe themselves, yet every night, after their baths, I would find their wet bath towels in a pile on the floor. I would then commence to bark at them to put the towels up, only to find later the towels piled in a clump on the toilet seat. Mumbling to myself about how lazy my boys were, I'd then hang the towels myself. Who knows how long this ritual would have continued if not for one night when something truly remarkable happened. In response to my barking about the towels, John, our youngest son, looked at me and had the wisdom to say, "Daddy, I don't know how to fold the towel." I stood there for a moment in stunned silence. It never occurred to me that I had to first teach them how to hang up a towel. Aren't we born with some sort of towel folding instinct? When I composed myself, the teacher in me kicked in and I conducted a towel folding/hanging lesson for the boys. I demonstrated and they practiced. And, as it turned out, this was no simple chore for them. They were smaller than the towels. It took them a few tries to get the corners together so they could hang the towel on the towel rod. Once they were able to do it successfully, I said, "Great! That's exactly what I want." Guess what? Those towels were rarely again left on the floor. So what is the moral of this story? You already know: it has nothing to do with towels.

Parents often expect children and teenagers to grasp concepts and skills they've not been taught or don't have the maturity for. I'm convinced that what parents often perceive as laziness, irresponsibility, or even defiance is in reality children's natural avoidance of what they don't know how to do. The towel experience taught me to think twice about some of my expectations and to make sure I'd taken the time to teach them what I expected of them. Sometimes I work with parents who expect their children to function like adults in children's bodies, which leads to on-going negative parent-child dynamics.

The mature parent fulfills his or her teaching responsibility through conscious use of the following strategies: routines, modeling, instruction, rules and consequences, work, and play.

Routines

Consistent routines bring order to children's lives and meet needs for continuity and security. Routines reduce anxiety and teach children how to bring order and organization to their own lives. Routines also instill healthy habits and some degree of self-control. Where there is lack of routine, there is usually too much chaos, reactivity, and stress. This atmosphere increases insecurity and anxiety in children and fails to teach them to organize their lives. Establishing consistent routines requires strong leadership from mature parents.

Modeling

Modeling may very well be the most powerful way that parents influence their children in the long term. For this reason, mature parents are highly conscious of what they are teaching through living. I remember an episode with our oldest son, Graham, when he was fourteen. I was extremely upset about something he'd done. I blew up and was harsh and disrespectful toward him. After we retreated to our respective corners, I realized I had just acted like the child in the grown-up body. I also realized the opportunity was not lost to model for him how to be an adult by taking responsibility for my behavior. I could still admit my loss of control and apologize. Despite still being quite upset with him, I decided modeling how to take responsibility was the priority. I went to him and in a rational, respectful tone, said, "Graham, even though I was upset with you, I truly regret my loss of control and what I said to you, and I sincerely apologize. We'll talk about what upset me later." A short while later, Graham approached me and said, "Dad, I know what I did was wrong and I'm really sorry." I doubt seriously that I would have gotten a willing apology from Graham had he not just seen his father model it for him.

Immature parents tend to be guided by the unconscious principle of "Do as I say, not as I do," and still don't understand why their child doesn't respect them. Mature parents are highly conscious of the principle that actions have to be consistent with words and expectations to have credibility. It still amazes me when people think they can demand respect from their children simply because they hold the exalted title of "parent."

Mature parents attempt to be a positive model for their children in the following areas:

- Personal responsibility and pro-activity
- Life principles and values
- Self-acceptance and independent thinking
- Managing feelings
- Interpersonal skills
- Assertiveness
- Respect
- Positive thinking

Instruction

If we are to empower our children, we have to teach them certain insights and skills that require a little formal instruction. We have to take time to talk about values and why they're important. Likewise we need to set aside time and energy to teach our children how to make a bed or a sandwich, how to introduce themselves, or how to express anger. The mature parent is able to recognize, in some of a child's negative behavior, the skill or insight deficit reflected by the behavior and to find the teaching moment.

When it comes to instruction, a little knowledge of learning theory comes in handy. It's naïve to think you've taught your children how to do something by simply telling them what to do. To be effective, you must apply a few more steps:

- Explain the skill you want them to learn.
- Explain the importance or benefit of the skill.
- Demonstrate the skill.
- Have them practice the skill.
- Praise them when they apply the skill.

Applying these steps may seem mechanical and unnatural, but if you grasp these steps, you can incorporate them in a very natural way in your interactions with your children. When you apply these steps, you get much better results than when you just tell them what to do. When you find yourself saying, "I've told you a thousand times!" that's a sign that you're not using enough steps. I told my sons "a thousand times" to hang up their towels, but nothing changed until I demonstrated it for them and then had them practice.

When I work with pre-teens in counseling, I sometimes hand them a deck of cards comprised of age-appropriate feeling words with coinciding facial expressions. Then I tell them we're going to practice an important life skill – putting words to feelings. I ask them to pick the cards that best describe their feelings recently and to then tell me about those feelings. Most respond well and take seriously the task of picking the right cards. I watch the wheels turn as they search for words that match their feelings. They don't realize what this is teaching them, but I do. When this exercise is repeated enough, I see progress when children come to a session, sit down, and launch right into a conversation about feelings without the cards. It's a simple activity, but it incorporates perhaps the most important step in a learning process: practice.

My experience working with foster children provided me a dramatic illustration of how skill deficient children can be when deprived of basic instruction and how these deficits can explain negative behavior. It's important to never assume children know how to do something unless they have been instructed according to sound learning theory.

I have directed children and teenagers on such skills as how to ask a teacher for help, what to say to a bully, how to break up with a boyfriend, how to talk to yourself when you're down, how to say no, or how to apply for a job. The list of skills children need instruction for is endless. Mature parents are attuned to their child's need for instruction and spot the opportunities to provide this kind of teaching. Where an insightful parent sees knowledge and skill deficits in some of a child's negative behavior, the immature parent just sees willful, bad behavior and reacts punitively.

Mature parents have an advantage when it comes to instructing their children, because they come equipped with necessary insights and skills. Some parents are no more insightful or skilled than their children. If you're a parent who feels you lack the insight to understand your child's behavior and the skills to teach your child, join the crowd and take heart. You can learn through counseling and through the abundance of parenting literature available. Again, the issue is not how much you know; it's how much you're willing to learn.

Rules and Consequences

The word "discipline" comes from an ancient Latin term meaning "to teach" or "to train." The mature approach to discipline aims purely at teaching. Sound discipline is administered rationally and respectfully with the learning goal in mind. Children and teenagers need a fairly structured environment consisting of a basic set of rules and expectations in order to develop personal responsibility. To make the rules and expectations stick, the mature parent applies consequences strategically. The two types of consequences that, when used effectively, promote the best learning in children and teens are "natural" and "logical," because they make sense to the child. When the consequences are applied reactively and seem arbitrary or illogical, children will focus more on the over-reaction of their parent than on their own responsibility.

Here are a few examples of natural and logical consequences:

Natural Consequences

- When a child refuses to wear a coat when it is cold outside, getting cold does the teaching.

- When a child mistreats a bicycle causing it to break, not being able to ride it or having to pay for the repair does the teaching.

Logical Consequences

- When a teen comes in past curfew, losing the privilege of going out the next night does the teaching.

- When a teen misuses a phone, losing the privilege of the phone does the teaching.

One of our sons, while in the eighth grade, was suspended from the school bus for three days due to misbehavior. He came to me the afternoon of his suspension wanting to know what time we would be leaving for school the next morning, assuming I would be driving him. As I was already aware of the situation, I was a step ahead of him. Now I could have yelled at him, told him how ashamed of him I was and said to him, "No son of mine is going to act that way! You're grounded for two weeks!" Instead, I told him calmly I had no intention of driving him, and since he had lost his ride, his options were to get up earlier and ride his bike or get up much earlier and walk. His school was just barely within a reasonable distance of both. Either option required considerable effort on his part to arrive to school on time. He chose to ride his bike to school. This logical consequence convinced him to control his behavior on the bus, which was my main goal.

I'm confounded by parents who complain about having to nag and argue with their kids to complete chores, clean their rooms, pick up their clothes and toys, or do their homework. Many parents believe they're helpless when, in fact, they hold all the cards. Mature parents ask their child respectfully to do what they expect. Then, if their child does not follow through within a reasonable period of time, they calmly and firmly proclaim that all other activities will cease until the expectation is met. These activities might include privileges like access to the television, phone, video games, computer, toys, play of any kind, seeing friends, or use of the car. These are all activities that should be privileges to which parents control access. Then, when the expectation is satisfactorily met, the mature parent allows the child to resume normal activity The immature parent engages in power struggles with the child. The mature parents know who holds the cards and plays them strategically.

Immature parenting tends to be either too inconsistent or too rigid in relation to expectations and rules. The immature response to a child's negative behavior varies from permissiveness, denial, and enabling on one end of the spectrum to high reactivity, shaming, nagging, yelling, arguing, and punitive use of consequences on the other end. The net effect of this type of parenting instills in children irresponsibility, anxiety, insecurity, shame, disrespect, powerlessness, and resentment. Mature parents can tell you what they're teaching their child in their approach to discipline. They understand what type of consequences are developmentally appropriate for the age of their child. They use leverage strategically in order to instill personal responsibility while at the same time communicating love and respect.

Work

One of the many important gifts parents can give their children is a solid work ethic. I've always advocated that children should be assigned household chores congruent with their developmental capabilities. We required our sons to make their beds and keep their rooms straight as soon as they were physically able. The list of basic chores expanded as they got older. We taught them that in the Kelly family everyone contributes to making life run well. As their list expanded, so too did their work habits. They weren't just handed money. They understood that, in most cases, they had to earn it. We explained to our sons, well in advance, to foster independence, that when they turned sixteen they would be responsible for providing their own spending money for entertainment, gas, and incidentals. They took the news in stride because they were already oriented in that direction, and to them it was a foregone conclusion. By the time they were twelve, they were used to seeking odd jobs to make money, and by age fifteen both had secured part-time jobs. Today they are strong, independent young men who know how to work hard and have been successful, in large part, because of their work ethic.

I often observe parenting that is too child-centered. This type of parenting over-protects, over-indulges, enables irresponsibility, does too much for while expecting too little from children. Children, just like adults, need to feel productive to gain a sense of self-worth. They pay a high price when they don't develop a strong work ethic. It is disconcerting to see eighteen-year-olds who haven't worked a day in their lives and have the maturity of fourteen-year-olds.

The process of learning how to manage work responsibilities is essential to maturation. Here are a few elements inherent in learning how to work:

- Time management
- Accountability to a boss
- Delaying gratification
- Frustration tolerance
- Interpersonal skills
- Focus and task completion
- Confidence and independence

Remember the old adage: "Give a man a fish and you feed him for a day. Teach him how to fish and you feed him for a lifetime." The same is true when you teach your child how to work.

Play

Just as learning how to work facilitates a child's maturation, so too does play provide a rich curriculum for a child's development. Since I've had the opportunity to observe our sons develop from infants to adolescents to adults, it is vividly clear that play has been a powerful teacher in their lives.

Since they were little boys, they played games with friends – usually some kind of ball game. In the beginning, the games didn't last very long because one of the kids would break a rule. As the conflict escalated, one kid would yell and scream, another would push and shove, or one would throw the ball at another. Finally, the ball's owner would grab the ball and stomp off. Game over!

As time went on, I noticed the games lasted a little longer and longer. As conflict arose, I observed signs of budding self-control and even some crude attempts at conflict resolution. It took a while before they could actually complete a game as planned. At some point, I was marveling at the comparison between where they started and what I was now observing – self-control, compromise, conflict resolution, teamwork, and even sportsmanship at the end as they told each other "good game" and shook hands.

In the early part of my career, during my work with teenage foster children in group homes, I observed what results when kids are deprived of normal play experiences in their childhoods. Watching those sixteen-year-olds try to play a game together was like watching six-year-olds. It was a dramatic display of their immaturity, reflective of the void of play in their lives. We simply don't realize how much positive learning takes place during play.

Apart from the array of social skills that play teaches, play is vital also to the development of creativity and problem solving in children. Ultimately, play is a powerful human need. Life is to be enjoyed and we experience much of our joy through the various forms of play we cultivate. Often, when I work with depressed children and teens, I find a lack of fun activities in their lives. Learning how to play during childhood lays groundwork for positive relationships, creativity, and the skills to maintain emotional balance.

Mature parents understand the importance of play and take a strategic approach by providing, encouraging, and supporting a child's exposure to a range of play activities. This includes the parents' active participation in some of these activities. Sometimes, I find that immature parents are so lost in their own problems, that their child's play needs are neglected. I'm saddened when I see a child who is unable to identify fun interests and parents who aren't taking action. These parents usually exhibit a void of fun activities in their own lives; parents who don't know how to play are hard-pressed to teach children how to enjoy life.

Meeting your child's play needs doesn't require money, but it does require resourcefulness, creativity, and time. Mature parents can identify what they do consciously and strategically to promote play in their child's life. They also understand there's no better way to bond with children than to take the time to play with them.

Conclusion

I have tried in this section to capture the essence of a parent's responsibilities and some of the distinctions between mature and immature parenting. There are different paradigms for framing the role of a parent, but to me, there is none better than **"nurturer/teacher."** Some parents unconsciously assume the role of friend, but wind up being enablers of irresponsibility because they fail to hold their children accountable. Other parents assume the role of boss and put all of the emphasis on their authority and their child's obedience. These parents succeed at gaining control of their child on the surface, but fail to have a deeper more positive influence. Both the "friend" and the "boss" fall short of fostering their child's growth. The "nurturer/teacher" strikes the right balance.

I believe, however, that there is something that parents are not responsible for in the lives of their children – the outcome. As we have become more child-centered, too many parents have assumed the responsibility for making their children happy and ensuring their success. This self-imposed pressure creates an anxiety that is counter-productive to parenting. Dwelling on the outcome communicates fear rather than trust and confidence and is usually expressed in the form of enabling or micro-managing. There are too many variables outside parents' control for them to assume complete responsibility for their child's success and happiness. Our responsibility, as parents, is to nurture and teach, communicate trust and confidence, trust life to do its own share of the teaching, and then to let go.

Self-Acceptance Applied to Parenting

*I plant the seeds of a positive sense of self
and fundamental self-acceptance in my child.*

When I see children in therapy, I spend almost as much time with parents as I do the child. Family systems theory asserts that in most cases a child's problems are symptomatic of problems in the family dynamic. Often, where I find a depressed, anxious, angry, or insecure child, I find a parent exhibiting the same symptoms. I have also seen children's issues resolve once their parents have addressed and resolved their own mental health problems. I cannot emphasize enough how important it is for parents to have a handle on their own lives before they can instill the traits they desire in their children. If parents recognize that their child is exhibiting similar issues to their own, they should make seeking professional help for themselves a first priority.

It's a challenge for an insecure parent to plant the seeds of fundamental self-acceptance in a child. The foundation of a positive sense of self in parents equips them to differentiate between their own identity and their child and allows them to view the child with the necessary objectivity. Without this foundation, parents are more likely to unconsciously view their child as an extension of themselves, distorting the parent-child dynamic. When we see our children as extensions of ourselves, we unconsciously need them to be the source of our happiness, identity, and self-worth. When we are dependent on our children in this way, we rise and fall too much on their experience and our own needs blind us to what they need from us.

When children are extensions of a parent's sense of self, they are often given messages to be perfect and to be the best at everything. They are taught to focus on image, to impress people, and to orient to what others think. Because they can't be perfect, they're subject to their parents' criticism, disapproval, and disappointment. The immature parent takes the child's negative moods, flaws, mistakes, and negative behaviors personally because these problems are viewed as a reflection on the parent. This triggers defensive reactions from the parent and blocks this parent from responding consciously and strategically to the needs of the child. I have worked with many adult clients who were programmed to believe that it was their responsibility to make their parents proud and happy when they were children.

Another version of the lack of differentiation between parent and child is enmeshment, a dynamic that occurs when a parent feels completely responsible for the child's happiness and consequently over-protects and over-indulges the child. This unhealthy attachment is also marked by the parent's deep dependency on the child's love and approval. This parent's enabling of the child fails to teach the child personal responsibility. I have worked with many parents who agreed they needed to hold their child more accountable but, when the time came, could not bear making their child unhappy or feeling their child's disapproval. The irony, of course, is that, in many cases, the result of this type of parenting is a deeply unhappy child.

With healthy differentiation, mature parents understand their child cannot make them happy, nor can they make their child happy. Without unconscious dependency clouding the relationship, parents can view their children clearly as the unique individuals they are. The clearer a parent's view is of the child, the more targeted one's nurturing and teaching can be. One size doesn't fit all when it comes to raising children. Different children need different approaches. Most importantly, when we see our children objectively, we can better recognize and affirm who they are as human beings – their unique personality traits, interests, and abilities. Without this healthy differentiation, we unconsciously want to mold them in our image.

Rickie's dad was a good athlete and loved sports. He wanted Rickie to be an athlete too, and he put a lot of pressure on Rickie to be involved in several sports. Rickie's heart was never in sports, but he would participate to please his dad. However, Rickie's lack of passion and commitment frustrated and disappointed his father. Not only did Rickie grow up believing he let his father down, but he also denied and repressed an important aspect of who he was – an artist.

Sarah was an introverted child who enjoyed time to herself and reading. She had two good friends, but was not interested in much socializing. Her mother was an extravert whose priority was her social life. Her mother felt something was wrong with Sarah and would push her to socialize more. Sarah could sense how worried her mother was about her. She could hear her mother's subtle messages of lack of acceptance of her personality which, in turn, created insecurity in Sarah.

Jeff's father was a high-powered businessman. He believed the purpose of a college degree was to enable one to pursue a lucrative career. When Jeff told his father he wanted to major in education to become a teacher, Jeff's father would not hear of it. He told Jeff he was unwilling to pay for college unless Jeff chose a degree with more income potential.

One of the functions of nurturing is to be a mirror to the child – to identify and to affirm for the child the positive traits he possesses that he can't recognize in himself. This is one of the timeless themes in the classic movie, *The Wizard of Oz*. The Wizard helped the Tin Man, who believed he didn't have a heart, see the evidence of his compassion. He showed the Lion, who believed himself to be a coward, the obvious existence of his courage. He revealed to the Scarecrow who believed he didn't have a brain, the many signs of his intelligence. Mature parents practice this kind of wizardry by focusing on, validating, and affirming the unique aspects and strengths of their children. The adults foster the emergence of who their children are created to be, rather than attempting to create their children in their own image.

Jack Canfield, noted author and speaker on the subject of self-esteem, tells the story of working with teenage boys in a correctional facility. In one group meeting, he asked each boy to identify one thing he was good at. Most of the boys struggled to come up with something positive, but one of the boys didn't hesitate. He said, "The only thing I'm good at is robbing banks." Canfield didn't miss a beat. He said, "Let's list the traits required to be a good bank robber." He went on to recognize this boy for being adept at organizing, problem-solving, observation, and leadership.

On the day one of our sons came home from school and announced his fourth grade teacher called him lazy, I looked him in the eye and said, "You are not to believe that. I know how much effort you put into many things!" I was emphatic because of my acute awareness of the power certain messages have on children. Because immature parents live too unconsciously and reactively, they often shame their children repeatedly. They have little awareness of the damage they're doing. Of course, many of these parents were on the receiving end of the same shaming messages from their parents and are now parenting according to their unconscious learning.

Parental messages are powerful influences on a developing child's core beliefs. When children receive a certain message about themselves repeatedly, they eventually believe it and behave in accordance with the belief. On one level, the immature parent thinks that shame is correcting the child when, in reality, it is negatively programming the child. On another level, shame is an unconscious and destructive expression of a parent's negative feelings of anger, frustration, fear, disappointment, and helplessness.

Here are some examples of shaming messages:

You're hopeless.	You'll never learn.
You're irresponsible.	Don't be stupid.
You're lazy.	You're a trouble-maker.
You're a liar.	You're not trustworthy.
What's wrong with you?	You're a bad boy.
You don't care about other people.	You're incapable of . . .
You're a slob.	You're helpless.

Mature parents stay on the look-out for opportunities to affirm their child's true nature. Affirmations are most effective when they are expressed subtly, matter-of-factly, and based on hard evidence. When affirmations are exaggerated, over-dramatized, and lack evidence, they are less believable.

Here are some simple examples of effective affirmations:

- That was a really good idea you had. It shows your creativity.
- You really worked on that. It shows your conscientiousness.
- That was nice of you to invite her. It shows your kindness.
- I am impressed with how you solved that problem. It shows your intelligence.
- When you do that without me asking, it shows your helpfulness.
- You seem to have a real interest in art. Good for you.
- You seem to notice details. You're a good observer.
- I'm proud of you for taking responsibility.
- Your ability to entertain yourself and not need to be around people all the time is a good thing.
- Your friendliness really comes through.

Mature parents' consciousness and skill is particularly on display in the way they communicate when they're frustrated or angry and have to correct or to discipline their child.

Immature parent:	Your room is a pigsty. You live like a slob. When I come back, it better be cleaned up!
Mature parent:	I'm frustrated with the way your room looks. You can't go out to play or watch T.V. until you clean it up.
Immature parent:	You were mean to Bobby when you two were playing together. You're really selfish.
Mature parent:	I was disappointed in how you treated Bobby by not sharing your toys with him. The next time you have a friend over, you will have to share more or there will be a consequence.
Immature parent:	Your laziness and irresponsibility are driving me crazy. You don't follow through on anything that I tell you to do.
Mature parent:	I'm frustrated with your lack of follow-through. Since I want you to develop responsibility, I have a new ground rule. You have to complete your chores and your homework before you are free to do other things.
Immature parent:	You do so many stupid things without thinking. You're hopeless.
Mature parent:	You may have to learn some things the hard way until you learn how to stop and think first.

Parenting is inherently stressful at times. Immature parents allow the stress to take control of the messages they give their child.

Mature parents, under the same stress, maintain the consciousness necessary to give the constructive messages needed to guard their child's self-worth.

All children have abilities, interests, and positive traits in them that sometimes lay dormant and are hard to spot. It takes an unobstructed view and an insightful eye for parents to see and to nurture these latent strengths. The parents who see their children with this kind of clarity are the ones who cultivate within their children the seeds of a positive sense of self and fundamental self-acceptance. These parents are the adults in the room.

Independent Thinking Applied to Parenting

I encourage my child to trust his own thinking.

A fellow therapist I know tells the story of his not liking certain foods as a child and his mother preaching that he didn't know what was good for him. The problem was he got the message, "You don't know what's good for you," in a variety of ways over a period of years until he believed it. He went on to explain that he's spent most of his adult life learning how to trust his own thinking and, to this day, it doesn't come naturally.

Identifying, validating, and trusting our own thinking are keys to developing identity and maturity. Because so much of our world discourages independent thinking, it is imperative for parents to encourage children to trust their own thinking. Parents have to walk a fine line in giving this guidance. On the one hand, parents are responsible for teaching their children a positive set of principles and values to live by, while on the other hand allowing them to question and to make up their own minds. For example, imagine a twelve-year-old child questioning one of his parent's firmly-held religious beliefs. An immature parent would likely respond defensively by telling the child that he is wrong for questioning the belief and conveying that there are certain things that he is not allowed to question. A mature parent, however, would convey encouragement and respect for the question. The mature parent might first take a listening approach and ask the child what is motivating the question and encourage discussion based on what's on the child's mind. When mature parents explain a belief to a child, they avoid being coercive and leave the explanation with the child to consider.

One of our sons was born asking "why?" and would challenge me about some of my rules and decisions, particularly those that related to him. When he would question me, he usually had at least one good point to make, but his teenage delivery was a bit too defiant for me. I wanted to encourage his independent thinking and, at the same time, teach him how to present his case assertively rather than aggressively. I told him he made some good points, but that I found it difficult to consider them because of his tone. I explained if he approached me rationally and respectfully, I would hear him out. Little by little he learned how to make his case respectfully. When he did approach me properly, I would intentionally modify my decision some in his favor to both encourage his independent thought and reward his approach. Today, as an adult, he is an independent thinker and skillfully assertive.

It is common in my work with families to encounter highly authoritarian parents whose focus is on being right and in control. This dictatorial approach can so disempower children and teenagers that it can have lasting, negative developmental effects. This parenting approach can insidiously program a child to be a people-pleaser and to mistrust his own thinking. I see many grown-ups who were recipients of autocratic parenting and who now can't think for themselves.

We want our children to realize they possess one of the most powerful tools on earth – their mind and its ability to think. But to maximize its potential, a mature parent has to know how to cultivate its use.

Years ago, one of the belts on my riding lawn mower slipped off of its pulley slightly. Since it had not come off totally, I felt that if I could just get the right leverage, I could force it back on without having to take everything apart. I fought with that mower for an hour. After a while, one of our sons, who was twelve at the time, came out to see what was going on. He studied the situation for a minute and then went into the garage and came back with a tool I hadn't thought to use. He held that tool in just the right position, and together we slipped the belt back on in a matter of seconds. I marveled at his ability to think through the problem and solve it and didn't miss the opportunity to tell him. From that point, I was more conscious of looking for openings to ask for our sons' opinions. I wanted them to believe in the validity of their own thinking and the power of their minds.

Just as the immature parent wants his child to be like him, he also wants his child to think like him. As a parent, I tried to distinguish between my expectations of our sons' behavior and their freedom to have and to express their opinions and feelings, as long as it was done properly. They were allowed to disagree and to object, but they still had to comply. Authoritarian parents who squash disagreement discourage independent thinking and hurt their children in the long run. There are a hundred ways a parent can say unconsciously to a child, "You shouldn't think that way." There is a significant difference between the message, "You don't know what's good for you," and the message, "You're free to dislike the broccoli, but you still have to eat it."

Because children in grown-up bodies don't trust their own thinking, they're poorly equipped to cultivate independent thinking in their children. Here are examples of messages immature parents give their children that program them to mistrust their thinking.

> You're a knucklehead.
> Where did you get a crazy idea like that?
> You must have mush for brains.
> You never think.
> Is there anybody home in there?
> You only know how to make bad decisions.
> Don't think that way.
> You don't know what's good for you.
> Don't question me. Just do what you're told.
> Sometimes you can be so dumb.

These messages might seem comical, but they have the power to be debilitating to children and teenagers over time. Immature parents can make statements like these with an utter lack of awareness of their damaging effects. Because mature parents understand the power of their message and the goal of cultivating independent thinking, they are alert to opportunities to give their children these kinds of messages:

> You have a good head on your shoulders.
> That was a great idea.
> You really thought that one through.
> That was a good decision.
> That was creative thinking.
> You really used your brain on that one.
> I can tell you've really been thinking about this.
> You really made a good point.
> That's a good question.
> I trust you to figure it out.
> That decision was a mistake, but I trust you to learn from it.

Here are a few other simple strategies for cultivating your child's independent thinking:

- Look for opportunities to ask the following questions:

  > What do you think about that?
  > How do you feel about that?
  > What do you like?
  > What do you want?
  > What do you believe?

- Practice active listening:

  > Allow your child at times to steer the conversation in the direction he or she wants to go so as not to dominate the discussion.

> Try to understand the true meaning of what your child is trying to say.
>
> Look for opportunities to validate your child's thoughts and feelings and avoid trying to change them.

- When possible, give your child some input into decisions you make that affect him or her.

- Take time to explain your rationale for some of your decisions to your child.

- Take time to explain some of your guiding values and principles to your child.

- Give your child the freedom to make some developmentally appropriate choices and decisions.

- Give your children room to solve some of their own problems and convey confidence in their ability to do so.

- Convey confidence in your child's ability to learn from mistakes.

- Model trust in the validity of your own thinking.

Many mental health problems are rooted to some degree in a lack of orientation and trust in one's own thinking. More than ever, our children grow up in a world that bombards them with external stimuli and immerses them in more information than they can assimilate. This puts them at risk to take too many cues from the outside world, which inhibits growth of independent thinking. For this reason, parents can't leave this part of their children's development to chance. Mature parents understand the significance of this issue and are conscious of their strategies for encouraging their children to think for themselves.

Conscious Feeling Applied to Parenting

I help my child process and manage feelings consciously.

Children's inherent temperaments will determine to some degree how they process and express feelings. However, if you want a general predictor as to how your children will manage their feelings, particularly the negative ones, when they grow up, look no further than the way you handle your own. Nowhere are the effects of modeling more powerful than in this aspect of a child's learning.

Carolyn entered counseling shortly after her husband informed her that he was in love with another woman and wanted a divorce. She expressed concerns about her seventeen-year-old daughter, Natalie, who was aware of the situation. Carolyn wanted me to meet with Natalie to make sure she was OK. I asked this mother if she had talked with her daughter about how she was feeling and Carolyn admitted, "We don't really do that in our family." When I asked Carolyn what she herself was going through, her response was surreal. She talked about it as if we were discussing the weather. She seemed so emotionally disconnected from what was happening that it alarmed me. She was unable to express her feelings. I could see the pain in her eyes, but she could only say things like, "I suppose I should have seen it coming. We haven't been close for a while. I know he hasn't been happy. I worry about him." It was a troubling display of denial and repression of powerful feelings. Yet, what was even more troubling was that my session with her daughter Natalie was a mirror image of my session with Carolyn. Natalie exhibited the same detached stoicism as her mother. One of the unspoken rules to live by in this family was, "Don't feel." A few follow-up sessions with Carolyn revealed how she learned this rule in her family when she was a child. Now, sadly, she was passing this legacy on to her daughter.

Children need mature guidance to learn how to process and manage feelings effectively. When this learning is left to chance or is in the hands of an immature parent, the odds are against a good outcome. I have witnessed parents yell at their children to stop yelling. I have watched parents engage in arguments and petty debates with their children in which I could barely distinguish between parent and child. When it comes to managing feelings in parenting, the "Do as I say, not as I do" approach fails miserably.

Immature and unconscious parenting is usually teaching children to let defensive instincts take over in dealing with negative feelings – fight or flight.

Fight	Nagging	Mocking
	Arguing	Blaming
	Yelling	Threatening
	Shaming	Criticizing
	Lecturing	Being sarcastic
	Hitting	
Flight	Withdrawing	Passively resisting
	Not talking	Manipulating
	Leaving	Avoiding
	Denying	Placating
	Repressing	Ignoring

Not only does a parent's poorly managed feelings teach a child how to be reactive and defensive, the negative energy expressed is also hurtful and damaging to the child. One painful memory I have is of an episode from years ago when I was having a stressful day and not coping well. Catherine and I were in the midst of a tense conversation and one of our sons, who was seven at the time, kept pawing at me and interrupting me. Out of nowhere, I looked down at him with fire in my eyes and let forth this primal growl – the kind a wild animal would make just before an attack. He completely froze with a look of terror on his face I will never forget, just before he melted into tears. I swept him up in my arms and told him how sorry I was and that I would never frighten him like that again. Fortunately, this incident was an extreme exception to the rule of emotional safety that existed in our family. I say this because when you're a flawed human being, mistakes are inevitable in parenting. You're allowed a few of those as long as they are rare exceptions to the rule. When expressions like that become the rule, you can bet it's doing damage. I have worked with many people who had to live with constant fear as children.

Parents must be aware that feelings within families are contagious. In most cases, where there is an anxious or depressed child, there is an anxious or depressed parent. Likewise, generally happy parents have generally happy children. Because mature parents understand this principle, they make their own well-being and taking good care of themselves priorities. Immature parents tend to neglect their own mental and emotional health, and in doing so create a troubling emotional climate for their children. Subsequently, they are prone to make some damaging mistakes in how they deal with their feelings. They sometimes blame their children for their stress or unhappiness, or they sometimes lean on and confide in their children for support. One mother told me recently, with pride, that her teenage daughter sometimes confronts her husband, the daughter's father, for not treating Mom better. This woman thought it was good that her daughter was so sensitive to her hurt that she would defend her against her husband. She was completely unaware of how unhealthy it was for her daughter to be playing this role and how it was hurting her daughter to feel responsible for her mother's happiness.

Mature parents have two primary goals related to feelings in family life: first, to process and to manage their own feelings consciously to create a healthy emotional climate, and second, to help their child learn to process and manage feelings consciously. To accomplish these two goals, practice and teach your children the following:

- Stress, to your child, the importance of expressing the more vulnerable types of negative feelings rather than allowing them to build up inside. Explain the benefits of expressing these feelings and the negative consequences of letting them build up.

- Avoid saying, "You shouldn't feel that way." Instead, teach your child that there are no wrong feelings. Human beings experience the full range of feelings. If we judge certain feelings, we condemn ourselves for having them, which then compounds them. Every day, I see people who feel ashamed or guilty for some of their darker feelings and then repress them. When we allow feelings, we are more open to listening to and to understanding them, which leads to resolving them. We are also more connected to ourselves when we allow ourselves to feel what we feel.

- Practice and teach an array of feeling words. Empowered people can articulate how they feel and why they feel the way they do. In most cases, negative feelings begin to resolve by simply giving them accurate words and allowing them to be felt. A good feeling vocabulary empowers us to make ourselves better understood to others. When your children are upset, use the situation as an opportunity to help them identify the most accurate words to describe their feelings. The words you teach your children should, of course, be congruent with their level of maturity.

- Practice a simple but effective active listening skill called "reflecting feelings" when you sense your child is troubled about something. Say to him or her,

"It sounds like you're feeling ___ (fill in the blank) ___."

or

"Are you feeling _____?"

Examples:	Sad	Frustrated	Worried
	Lonely	Angry	Afraid
	Left-out	Disappointed	Nervous
	Hurt	Discouraged	Helpless

This is both a good way to teach a feeling vocabulary and to convey understanding and empathy. The sooner your children feel understood, the sooner their negative feelings will resolve.

- Look for opportunities to model, in a measured and strategic way, the expression of vulnerable feelings without burdening your children. There are appropriate times for a parent to admit to a child a hurt, a fear, or a sadness, for example, as part of the human experience. However, the expression of these vulnerable feelings should not put a child in the position of feeling responsible for them.

- Teach your child that the expression of anger is allowed, but with self-control. Since anger represents powerful emotional energy, we have to be patient and accept that developing children are works in progress when it comes to handling frustration and anger. Don't expect them to be little adults. Learn to spot their small steps of progress with frustration tolerance. The long-range goal is to teach your child how to express frustration and anger rationally and respectfully. Your child also needs help in identifying and expressing any vulnerable feelings the anger is defending. Some instruction is necessary when it comes to teaching children how to deal with anger, but again, how you handle your own anger will have the most influence on your child in the long run.

Annie was an eight-year-old girl whose parents were at their wits' end. When upset, Annie would have a total meltdown, screaming and crying sometimes for long periods. Her parents tried applying consequences to subdue her, but to no avail. Even Annie admitted her loss of control was a problem and felt ashamed about it. After a little dissecting, it was clear her worst meltdowns were triggered by a certain family dynamic. Her father had remarried and her new family was in the process of blending two sibling groups. She went from being the youngest of three to the youngest of five. The emerging sibling dynamic caused her to feel left out at times; she was getting lost in the shuffle. Certain situations would trigger a sense of rejection, loneliness, and helplessness, yet she had no ability to express these feelings in words. When I asked her what she felt during the meltdowns, she couldn't tell me. I then tried out some words for her, and together we agreed that the words that best expressed her feelings were hurt, sad, left-out, lonely, helpless, and angry. I had her practice expressing these feelings by using the incomplete sentence, "I feel _____ when _____." I then coached her parents in how to help her express these feelings in the early stage of a meltdown, and it worked. Annie learned, through instruction, how to control herself by expressing her emotional energy through effective words – one of life's most essential skills. Expressing her feelings effectively also enabled her parents to better understand her needs and to make sure she was more included, which also helped solve the problem.

When it comes to helping your children process and manage their feelings, don't expect quick results. Try to remember what you were capable of when you were their age. Processing and managing feelings skillfully requires a sophisticated level of cognitive-emotional functioning. This means we have to understand the slow nature of this kind of growth and be patient.

We have to trust that, if we plant and cultivate the necessary seeds and stay the course, growth will occur. Parents have a challenging responsibility to help their children learn how to process and manage feelings consciously. Those who parent with this awareness and with the necessary insight, skills, and patience are the adults in the room.

Positive Core Beliefs Applied to Parenting

I teach my child to think consciously and positively.

Earl Kelly, my father, was not highly educated, but was inherently wise. He grew up on a small dairy farm, milked cows every morning before he went to school, and eventually assumed ownership and operation of his parents' feed and dry goods store that became Kelly's Hardware. I guess you could say he was a businessman, but at heart he was a psychologist and philosopher. Dad was not an avid reader, but he loved inspirational literature. His favorites were among the classics of his day – *The Power of Positive Thinking*, *Think and Grow Rich*, and *How to Win Friends and Influence People*. Conversations with him were often interspersed with references from his reading. We jokingly referred to his musings as "Earl's pearls."

When I was growing up, we had a small chalkboard hanging in our kitchen for miscellaneous notes and messages. Almost every day, Dad would leave a brief thought for the day on the board before he left for work. They were the kinds of messages that most people would dismiss as clichés – "Make it a good day," "Look on the bright side," "You can do it," "Be kind." I can remember scoffing at some of them when I was a teenager. Little did I know that, while I thought I was dismissing those messages, I was being programmed by them.

Think about how much you still hear your parents' voices reflected in some of your thoughts, either consciously or unconsciously. I still hear my parents' voices. Lucky for me, they were mostly positive and uplifting. It's hard for me to imagine what my thoughts and beliefs would reflect had my parents' voices or messages been more negative. Your children will hear your voice for the rest of their lives. Will your messages serve to help sustain them or to inhibit them?

I'm sure you recognize the theme that runs through this section on parenting – the power a parent possesses to shape a developing child's learning. I've addressed how parents can influence their children's level of self-acceptance, ability to trust their own thinking, and skill to manage feelings effectively. Now add to the list how a parent influences the way a child thinks about life.

It gives one pause to consider how much power a parent has to condition a child's young mind. Often, the process of psychotherapy involves helping people re-program faulty and distorted thinking learned in childhood. Mature parents tend to be guided by conscious, healthy thinking they mindfully pass on to their children. Immature parents tend to be controlled by unconscious, negative programs they mindlessly teach their children.

There are four categories of thoughts and beliefs that have the strongest impact on our eventual success and happiness:

- Ourselves
- Other people
- Our future
- Life in general

I want to make clear that there are many competing influences on a child's way of thinking besides parents: other family members, peers, other influential adults such as teachers and coaches, the larger culture, and the media. Also, children sometimes internalize distorted interpretations of their experience that aren't a reflection of reality and are no one's fault. This means in most cases parents don't deserve all the credit nor all the blame for their child's programming. It is safe to say, however, that for most children, parents have the strongest influence.

What I have previously covered on helping children develop self-acceptance and independent thinking speaks adequately to how parents affect a child's beliefs about self. Therefore, in this section, I will focus on how parents influence their child's thoughts and beliefs in the areas of **other people, the future,** and **life in general.**

Other People

My experience working with foster children taught me how debilitating it can be to believe that you can't trust people. Most foster children learn, for good reason, to mistrust most people, as a result of having been abused or neglected at the hands of their own parents.

Eric Erickson's model of psycho-social stages of development emphasizes that the cornerstone to a child's healthy development is learning what he called "basic trust." I witnessed the psychological and emotional barriers within those mistrusting children and the negative and painful consequences of their "basic mistrust." Yet, children don't have to experience abuse or neglect to form problematic mistrust. Children's views of other people are shaped by a variety of influences, but mostly by their parents' modeling and by how they interpret their experience with parents and others.

The belief that you can't trust most people brings out the worst in us. The lenses of mistrust focus us on looking for evidence to confirm that others are against us, that their intent is malicious, that they will hurt us, take advantage of us, or that we can't rely on them. Mistrust keeps us on high alert and overly vigilant. At the slightest hint of danger, our defenses of fight or flight take over and sabotage our success and happiness. As with all core beliefs, we find evidence of what we're looking for and create self-fulfilling prophecies. This is not the world we want our children to live in. We want them to believe that, although there are, indeed, bad people out there, most people are good, well-meaning, and can be trusted. Everything in life tends to work better when we give people the benefit of the doubt as a result of basic trust.

Of course, the primary way a developing child learns basic trust is by growing up with mature adults who provide a consistently safe and loving environment. When the environment frequently evokes stress and fear, the child's trust in people is usually one of the casualties. Because mature parents understand that the stakes are high, they are acutely aware of being trustworthy – being safe, being honest, being consistent, and being reliable.

The kind of spoken messages a parent gives a child about other people is a secondary but powerful influence on a child's beliefs. These messages tend to be projections of a parent's level of trust or mistrust. Parents who are mistrusting are ill-equipped to teach trust to a child. Mature parents are highly conscious of how they want their child to view other people and what they say to orient their child in a positive direction. Mature parents tend to speak positively about other people to teach their children to see the good in people. Immature parents are more likely to openly gossip about and criticize people in the presence of their children. In doing so, they orient their children to view people negatively.

Another aspect of our view of other people has to do with our sense of belonging or connection to others. We are all at risk to conclude, "I don't belong," but children are particularly vulnerable. Mature parents teach a view that emphasizes our commonality and connection as human beings. Immature parents often teach an "us against them" view that emphasizes our differences and our separation. Obviously, we want to orient children to the view and belief that we're all connected. Here are some of the spoken and unspoken messages immature and mature parents give their children about other people.

Unconscious negative messages

> You can't trust most people.
> They'll take advantage of you.
> They only care about themselves.
> They don't care if they hurt you.
> You can't rely on other people.
> You can't get too close to other people.
> You have to keep your distance.
> They're not like us, and we're not like them.
> They have it made, and look at us.
> We don't have anything in common with them.
> They think they're better than us.
> We're better than them.
> We're right and they're wrong.
> They don't belong.
> We don't belong.

Conscious positive messages

> Most people are good people who have good intentions.
> Most people care about others.
> You can trust and rely on most people.
> Most people don't intend to hurt others.
> Most people are doing the best they know how to do.
> Most people behave negatively because of their own
>   problems.
> As humans, we're all in the same boat.
> No one has it made. We all have problems.
> We're all equal.
> What we have in common outweighs our differences.
> Risking getting close to people usually pays off.
> It's important to ask others for help at times.
> Everyone's point of view has some validity.
> Everyone has some good qualities, even if they're not
>   obvious.
> We are all connected.

Children who learn to mistrust, to be critical of, or to focus on their disconnection to others will, no doubt, live in a negative world, perhaps, their whole lives. These negative programs create self-fulfilling prophecies that leave one closed, cut-off, angry, and alone. Children who learn early to trust, accept, forgive, and see the positive in other people, stand a good chance of creating for themselves a positive world. They are more likely to take emotional risks, to be less defensive and more open, and to communicate positive energy that enables them to experience close relationships and a strong sense of belonging to others.

The Future

I have listened to some children and teens describe a dark picture of what they believed their future held. We all have a vision and beliefs about our future, but these beliefs tend to function, by and large, unconsciously. Children's visions and beliefs about their future stem from a limited picture of life as they know it. It's rare for them to imagine and expect something in their future outside of their previous frame of reference. Most children's expectations of the future will reflect their quality of life growing up, and they will create lives very similar to their parents' lives based on these unconscious imprints.

For these reasons, it's important for parents to help their children consciously imagine and expect good things for their future. In my work, I often witness the transference of parents' fears to their children. A parent's obsessive worrying, hand-wringing, and over-protection communicate two powerful messages: Bad things are going to happen and you can't handle it. When this goes on for long, children become programmed to believe those messages. Then parents bring them to me to treat them for anxiety and often don't see the connection between their own fears and their child's insecurities. This is just one more reason parents need to make their own well-being a priority in order to model and project confidence, empowerment, and hopefulness.

Here are the different kinds of spoken and unspoken messages children can receive from their parents about the future:

Unconscious negative messages

> Bad things are going to happen.
> You can expect the worst.
> What can go wrong will go wrong.
> You never get what you really want.
> If bad things happen, you won't be able to handle it.
> You don't have what it takes to succeed at _____ .
> Don't think too big, or you'll be disappointed.
> Always take the safe route.
> We have no control over our destiny.

Conscious positive messages

> Expect good things to happen.
> When bad things happen, you can deal with it.
> You can create your future and your happiness.
> You have what it takes to succeed.
> You can overcome obstacles.
> You have much to offer.
> Imagine achieving what you want.
> You will learn and grow from your experience.
> You can always make changes in your life.

Children who learn to be pessimistic about their futures are predisposed to anxiety and depression. They are more likely to opt for safety and avoid the risk-taking necessary for success. They will tend to expect to fail, which will inhibit their motivation and increase their odds of failure. Pessimism takes the form of negative energy that attracts more negatives into one's life.

Children who learn to be optimistic about their futures have less fear and more confidence in their ability to create what they want. They also have confidence to overcome the inevitable obstacles they will face. Their belief that they can succeed enhances their motivation and gives them the courage to take risks that increase the odds for success. The positive energy projected by their optimism attracts good things to them.

Life in General

We all have core beliefs about life in general. Our world view either enhances the quality of our lives or undermines our peace and happiness. Just as we pass on to our children our beliefs about other people and about the future, so, too, do we teach them, either consciously or unconsciously, how to think about life in general.

We have a choice as to what world we see. There is the world of darkness characterized by human pain and suffering, fear and ignorance, injustice, oppression, cruelty, bigotry, greed, poverty, illness and disease, and death. The world of light shines through in the form of love, sacrifice, generosity, friendship, adventure, mystery, accomplishment, community, creativity, redemption, growth, and nature's regenerative energy and beauty.

Children in grown-up bodies don't know they have a choice as to what world to see. Their view of life is dictated by their surroundings and by the six o'clock news. The adult understands that we can find whatever world we look for out there. Adults are certainly in touch with the painful realities in life but make a conscious choice to focus on the light because they know, in doing so, they are taking good care of their mental health.

Because we live in the age of the twenty-four hour news cycle that overwhelms us with information, it's more important than ever to teach our children how to view life consciously and positively. Certainly helping children see the good in most people leads them to a positive view of life in general. The next time there is a natural or man-made disaster, rather than focus on how cruel life can be, point out to your child how many people come forth to help those in need in times of crisis. We can help our children live in a positive world by teaching them to spot the random acts of kindness in their midst and by giving them opportunities to experience first-hand the joy felt in service to others.

We can shape children's views of life by exposing them to the richness found in the natural world. Children who learn how to access nature's pleasures are, to some degree, immunized from a dark view of life. They are more equipped to maintain a sense of mystery and awe toward life and to recognize the everyday miracles in their midst. Activities like camping, hiking, boating, fishing, gardening, caring for animals, collecting sea shells, counting stars, or savoring a sunset instill an understanding and reverence for the natural world and our connection to it.

Here are the different kinds of spoken and unspoken messages parents give their children about life in general.

Unconscious negative messages

Life is hard and cruel.

Life is all work and no play.

Life is about image.

Life is unfair.

Life is full of stress.

Life is about winning and achieving.

Life is about material possessions.

Life is about earning your ticket to heaven.

Conscious positive messages

Life is full of wonder and awe.

Life is about the simple pleasures.

Life is an adventure.

Life is about making a contribution.

Life is about love and relationships.

Life is about enjoying the journey.

Life is about learning and growth.

Life is about doing the best you can.

Teach your children to exercise the power they have to choose how they look at life. Today's children are at risk for developing a stressful view of life from being bombarded by information they're unequipped to process. They'll need increasing consciousness and skill to filter the information to which they're exposed.

Finally, most of our thoughts and beliefs manifest themselves primarily through our self-talk. Healthy self-talk is a very teachable skill to children and teenagers. Explain to your child that we all talk to ourselves and that there are right things and wrong things to say to ourselves in various situations. Look for opportunities to suggest some simple coping self-talk statements when your child is dealing with a stressor. Conscious self-talk is an essential life skill for success and happiness. Here are some random examples:

> I can deal with this.
> I don't have to be perfect.
> Everybody has problems.
> That look on her face may not have anything to do with me.
> I don't have to please everybody.
> I can learn from my mistakes.
> It's OK to be shy.
> It shows courage to admit I don't know something and to ask for help.
> It's OK if I'm not good at sports. I'm good with computers.
> My friends worry more about themselves than think about me.

What your children learn through your influence regarding how to think about themselves, other people, their future, and life in general will set the stage for their future success and happiness. How you care for them, what you model, and what you say to them systematically programs them to some degree. As flawed human beings, we shouldn't have so much power, but we do. The adult in the room parents with an acute awareness of this sacred responsibility.

Insight Applied to Parenting

I parent with insight and cultivate insight within my child.

If you parent under the premise that your child's behavior makes perfect sense and with the insight to understand your child's behavior, you're well on your way to mature and effective parenting. Your level of insight as a parent will often determine whether your response to your child is reactive or helpful. As I've already posited, most human behavior is explained by needs, personality, learning, and emotions. When it comes to parenting, there is an additional set of insights under the heading of child development necessary for success. This knowledge explains what children need, what they're learning, and what can be appropriately expected of them at each developmental stage. These insights are essential for strategic and effective parenting. The mature parent makes the extra effort to gain the necessary knowledge. There is an abundance of available literature dedicated to child development and parent effectiveness.

It goes without saying that a child's behavior will reflect, in part, the style and quality of parenting. When parents strike the right balance between nurturing and teaching, in most cases, the child's learning and growth proceed on a healthy track and behavior problems fall within a normal range. Parenting that over-indulges, over-protects, and enables tends to produce child behavior that is immature and irresponsible relative to the child's age. On the other hand, parenting that micro-manages or is autocratic tends to render child behavior that is either overly compliant or angry, dishonest, and defiant.

Both the enabler and the autocrat inhibit the child's development of a positive sense of self, independent thinking, personal responsibility, and life skills. In many cases, the enabler and the autocrat are acting out their own unresolved issues and faulty learning from childhood that block their effectiveness. But, I regularly counsel parents committed to becoming nurturer/teachers for their children and see their children's behavior improve as they take positive steps. If your child exhibits a pattern of negative behavior, the first question to ask yourself is, "What's the quality of my nurturing and teaching?" Revisit the section on nurturing and teaching in "Personal Responsibility Applied to Parenting." Children's negative behavior patterns are often symptoms of unmet needs, negative learning, or negative emotions. You can't solve behavior problems by controlling the symptoms. Insights and conscious strategies are required.

Remember Annie, the eight-year-old girl prone to lengthy screaming and crying episodes? Effectively responding to her problematic pattern required key insights, starting with her personality. Using the Myers-Briggs framework, she was highly extraverted and a strong feeler. Her extraversion meant she was driven to engage and interact with her new blended sibling group. Since she was the youngest of the five siblings by a few years, she was often excluded, leaving her to feel rejected and alone. The combination of her extraversion and feeling nature explained why all that emotional energy came pouring out. And, because her tantrums were so disruptive and lengthy, her parents made her stay in her room, which only further isolated her, increasing her distress. At eight years old, with such an emotive personality, Annie didn't have the tools to understand, calm, or control the intense emotional energy she could experience. Here are the insights that explain Annie's behavior:

Needs: Belonging, inclusion, interaction with siblings

Personality: Extraversion and Feeling – exclusion evokes high distress expressed through crying and screaming

Emotions: Left-out, lonely, hurt, sad, angry, and helpless

Learning: No verbal tools to express feelings

Developmental Stage: At eight years old, she cannot be expected to have good self-control, given the above factors. She will have to gradually learn. Progress will be slow and incremental.

Strategy:

- Listen to her with the intention of understanding, empathizing, and helping her to identify and verbalize her feelings.

- To meet her need for belonging, spend time with her when she is being excluded from the older siblings' play. Avoid isolating her at those times.

- Plan family activities that meet her need for belonging and interaction.

- Be patient with her slow growth.

- Observe and praise small steps toward self-control, like when she verbalizes her feelings or decreases the frequency and duration of her tantrums.

Parents without insight into child development expect children to exercise a level of self-control that stops misbehavior on a dime. Self-control is a challenge for all of us, much less children. Self-control is a complex skill we're still developing into our twenties and beyond. Rather than demand self-control, insight dictates we teach our children the small steps that comprise this rather sophisticated skill and then hold them accountable for practicing the steps.

Brandon was fourteen, highly intelligent, and very likable, yet he was bringing home poor grades, getting in trouble frequently for minor offenses like talking too much in class and not following through with his responsibilities. For example, when he was assigned a task, his parents would follow-up only to find he either never started or got distracted before he finished. He was also prone to losing and forgetting things. When he was confronted about his behavior, he'd react defensively and deny responsibility; sometimes he'd even outright lie. His parents and teachers were exasperated; they could see his ability and potential, but unfortunately, their lack of insight led them to view him as lazy, irresponsible, and deceitful. Their only approach was to shame and punish him for his misbehavior. They believed that the solution was for him simply to choose to be more responsible. Since Brandon had been shamed for years, the problem was compounded because he had internalized negative beliefs about himself; now some of his behavior was a reflection of those beliefs. Outwardly, he seemed happy-go-lucky, but internally struggled with anxiety and insecurities. Brandon woke up each day with the feeling he was going to mess something up, only he couldn't predict what and when.

Brandon's problem was a classic case of undiagnosed attention-deficit disorder. He was extremely impulsive, internally disorganized, highly distractible, and unable to sustain focus and concentration. He grew so weary of confrontation with his parents and teachers, he took to a deny and lie tactic in an effort to get them off his back.

Brandon's parents required a whole new set of insights in order to overhaul their view of him and their approach to parenting. To their credit, they were committed to learning, and as they applied effective strategies, Brandon improved his organization, task completion, and school performance, which led to a more positive family dynamic and newfound confidence in Brandon.

The following provide additional glimpses of a child's behavior making sense once insight is applied:

- Alex often skips his third period Geometry class. He feels lost in Geometry, but is ashamed to admit it. He'd rather risk the consequences of skipping class than experience feeling so lost and helpless in class. Alex needs help with Geometry.

- Vickie lies to her parents when she socializes with Sophie, who likes to go places Vickie isn't allowed. Vickie's need for Sophie's friendship trumps complying with her parents. Vickie's insecurities prevent her from saying "no" to her peers. She needs help with her insecurities.

- Jake's parents frequently catch him sneaking around to smoke and lying about it. No matter the consequences, Jake doesn't quit. Jake secretly experiences anxiety, and nicotine calms him. Jake needs help with anxiety.

- Most mornings, Bobby complains of a stomach ache and pleads to stay home from school. He drags his feet getting dressed and the whole way to the bus stop. His parents battle with him frequently to get him to leave on time. Unbeknownst to them, Bobby is bullied on the bus. Bobby needs help dealing with the bully.

- Tony is seventeen and frustrates his parents with his lack of initiative and responsibility. They expect him to get a part-time job and although he promises to, he never takes action. Tony's parents have resorted to nagging him, while continuing to give him money for things he wants. Sadly, Tony has never learned to take responsibility because he's never experienced real consequences. The enabling has to stop before Tony will accept more responsibility.

- Amy is fifteen and promiscuous with boys. Her parents are divorced and her father has never been a part of her life. She's deeply insecure about her self-worth. She needs the attention and approval of boys to make her feel lovable and worthy. Amy needs help with her insecurities.

- Katie secretly cuts on herself, but keeps the evidence covered up. She is ashamed and embarrassed by the behavior and the ugly cut marks. She is full of insecurity and stress and often feels overwhelmed. She's found when her anxiety gets out of control, her focus on cutting blocks the world out and temporarily calms her down. Katie needs help with her insecurity and anxiety.

I work with countless children and teens whose behaviors confound their parents. In most of these cases, parents are lacking critical insights that block their effectiveness. Parents with little insight often take their child's negative behavior personally, as if the misbehavior is aimed at them. They also tend to oversimplify their child's negative behavior as laziness, irresponsibility, disobedience, or defiance. The reality is, most of the time, their child's behavior makes sense based on needs, personality, learning, emotions, and developmental stage. With the insight to understand the meaning of a child's behavior, a parent can do the following consciously, strategically, and hence, maturely:

- Target and address underlying needs.

- Target and address underlying learning and skill deficits.

- Practice patience, acceptance, and affirmation in response to personality.

- Identify and offer empathy, support, and guidance in response to underlying feelings.

- Establish realistic expectations related to developmental stage.

- Target and apply the most effective consequences when they are needed.

Now let's turn our attention to the process of cultivating insight within children. We've all experienced that "ah haa" or "light bulb" moment that has ushered us into a new era of understanding of something that previously stumped us. Suddenly, this understanding equips us to deal with the old challenge more effectively. Moments like those can be deceiving, seeming to happen in an instant when, in reality, the insight had been incubating for a long time. The "ah haa" happens in a flash of receptivity coupled with a new experience or someone's creative explanation, but the seed of the new understanding was planted, maybe long ago, and cultivated over time. Once this new insight sprouts within us, it now guides us with no need for external direction.

Parents with little grasp of child development fail to understand the slow germination process of gaining insight. These parents expect to explain a concept to a child once, twice, or maybe three times for immediate results. Many of the insights they expect of their children aren't even available to them, developmentally, until their late adolescence at the earliest. Parents must accept that their job is to plant and cultivate the seeds of insight without getting to pick the fruit anytime soon.

Listen to the difference in these two exchanges between a parent and a seven-year-old son:

Parent:	I didn't like the way you were playing with Billy while he was here. You weren't sharing your toys with him. The next time he comes over I expect you to share more.
Son:	I don't want to let Billy play with my toys when I want to play with them!
Parent:	That means you're selfish and it's bad to be selfish!
Son:	I don't care!

Parent: If you keep being selfish, Billy won't want to play with you anymore.

Son: I don't care!

Parent: The next time I see you not sharing, you'll be punished!

- - -

Parent: I noticed while you were playing with Billy there were times when you weren't sharing your toys with him.

Son: I don't want to let Billy play with my toys when I want to play with them!

Parent: How would you feel if you were at Billy's house and he wouldn't let you play with his toys?

Son: (pause) Mad. (pause) Sad.

Parent: If you knew that Billy wasn't going to share his toys with you, would you want to play with him?

Son: (pause) No!

Parent: I think you want to be friends with Billy and I know you want to be kind and not hurt Billy's feelings. Can we agree that the next time he comes over you will consider his feelings by sharing more?

Son: I guess so.

Parent: Thank you. When the time comes, I'll remind you about our agreement.

One parent is attempting to control the child's behavior with coercion and shame. The approach is teaching the child to behave properly to avoid punishment. The other parent is attempting to influence the child's behavior by teaching empathy and appealing to his goodness. This approach is cultivating insight that will eventually guide him in the right direction. However, make no mistake, this parent will have to, repeatedly, reinforce this deeper perspective over time before the light bulb truly goes on.

Our sons had the great fortune of observing a highly dedicated and skilled teacher in their mother. Only a few times during their formal education did they wind up in the classroom of an incompetent teacher, but when it happened, the boys seemed to smell the lack of dedication a mile away, and before long they'd misbehave and find themselves in trouble with the teacher for whom they lacked respect. When these problems came to my attention, along with a consequence for their actions, I'd take the opportunity to discuss the situation. I can remember saying, many times, I understood how they felt, but that acting out disrespect only hurt them and not their teachers. One son had not been at college very long when he acknowledged he'd finally absorbed the lesson, once and for all, after an encounter with a particular professor he didn't respect, admitting his old way of reacting would only hurt himself. I had waited years for that moment.

Throughout those years, there were countless times when I wanted to find the shortcut to our sons "seeing the light." But I had to be satisfied to plant seeds and be patient. These days, in conversations, I marvel at how many light bulbs have come on and how insights now guide them.

Why do I have to eat this? Why do we have this rule? Why do I have to clean my room? Why can't I stay out later? Why do I have to do chores? Why can't I watch this? Why am I grounded? Why? Why? Why? It's the most common word you'll hear as a parent and still the best question a child can ask. The worst answer a parent can give to any "Why" is, "Because I said so." A why question is a golden opportunity to cultivate insight. Every why should be met with respect and taken seriously. Decisions, rules, and expectations should be based on sound values, principles, and purposes that children need to be taught. We want these underlying values and principles to guide them in the future.

"Because I said so!" teaches a child to simply do what he is told and does little to encourage independent thinking. "Because I said so!" is a disservice to a child's growth. In fact, the mature parent speaks to most "whys" before they are even asked.

It's generally true that when children and teens perceive parents' decisions, expectations, and rules to be arbitrary, they are less likely to accept them. Parents generally experience better cooperation from their children when they take the time to explain their rationale for their decisions. Even if children dislike or disagree with a parent's rationale, they feel respected by a parent's effort to explain. When they know there are objective reasons for decisions, expectations, and rules, they take them less personally and respond less defensively.

When parents look for opportunities to invest time to explain how life works, on many levels they're laying the important groundwork for their child's future maturity. Topics such as why people behave the way they do, how our own behavior affects other people, and why certain values and principles lead to success and happiness contain essential insights children will eventually rely on to navigate their journey.

For example, I've worked with many children and teenagers who have been the target of bullying. The effects of bullying can inflict lasting pain. One of the small ways I work to lessen the negative impact of the bullying experience is by planting seeds of insight about the bully. Bullies, I explain, are kids with problems and insecurities who need attention; they put others down in an attempt to impress people and feel good about themselves. I add that oftentimes bullies are themselves being bullied, maybe even by their parents, and are taking their anger out on others. These insights don't solve the problem, but if the victim can see the bully in a new light, it lessens the credibility of the bully and thus the power of the long-term impact. We all stand to benefit from these insights since we all, at least occasionally, encounter petty tyrants.

Parents who qualify as the adults in the room understand that life and parenting are complex and have the insights necessary for effective parenting. These tools equip them to see below the surface of behavior to spot the nurturing and learning needs of their children. Their perceptiveness informs their best parenting strategies. Likewise, their deeper understanding of life's complexities equip them to plant and cultivate the seeds of insight that will one day empower their children.

Assertiveness Applied to Parenting

I model and teach my child assertive communication.

Listen to these two different conversations between a parent and a thirteen year-old son, and guess which parent is the adult in the room.

Son: Can I spend the night at Robbie's tonight?

Parent: No!

Son: Why not?!

Parent: Because you have to be at your youth group activity at 8:00 in the morning and you won't get enough sleep tonight at Robbie's.

Son: Yes, I will! That's so stupid and unfair!!!

Parent: You're the one that's stupid for talking to me like that! You're grounded!!

- - -

Son: Can I spend the night at Robbie's tonight?

Parent: I want you to be well rested and energetic for your youth group activity in the morning, and I doubt that you and Robbie will get much sleep tonight. I'm sorry, but the answer is no.

Son: I'll get enough sleep! That's so stupid and unfair!!

Parent: (in a rational tone) You're allowed to disagree with me and be angry at me and you can tell me in the right tone of voice, but you're not allowed to be disrespectful. I can promise you'll never get your way with me when you talk to me like that. Now, how about you practice telling me that you disagree with me and you're mad at me in a respectful tone of voice.

Son: (more rationally) I disagree with you and I'm mad at you.

Parent: That's better.

Take a minute and imagine your children as adults one day. Picture them in communication with a spouse, with colleagues, or a boss at work. Envision how you want their communication to sound. Most parents hope to see their adult children as confident in their thoughts, feelings, and wants. We envision our grown children expressing themselves directly, rationally, and respectfully. Likewise, we picture them listening to others with an open mind. We don't imagine them communicating passively, aggressively, reactively, or defensively, but rather with self-awareness and skill. Ask yourself if you practice and model the communication skills you envision for them.

Know that the best predictor of how your children will communicate as adults is how you communicate with them today. If they're to communicate assertively, they will need some instruction, since defensive communication is more instinctive. Assertive communication is comprised of higher consciousness and learned skills.

Teaching assertiveness requires different approaches for different children. Strong-willed, outspoken children are at risk for communicating too aggressively when they grow up. These children require an approach that encourages their independent nature but harnesses their thoughts and feelings into constructive assertiveness. Hopefully, life lessons and their natural consequences, along with a parent's strategic use of logical consequences, will be enough to point these children in a positive direction. Parents of aggressive children must make clear to them that they will not get what they want unless they make the effort to express thoughts and feelings rationally and respectfully. Parents with aggressive children must avoid overreacting to their child's behavior in order to model for the child the skills to be learned. When this child takes even a small step toward communicating thoughts, feelings, and wants with self-control and skill, his or her efforts should be heard, validated, and rewarded. I speak from personal experience as I had to apply these approaches with our own strong-willed son, who has learned how to harness his personality and assert himself skillfully.

On the other hand, a naturally compliant child can be at risk of becoming a people-pleaser, which is also problematic. Although a parent may enjoy the peace of a compliant child, there can still be cause for concern if a child is too easy to control. As parents, we want to see signs of an independent will. Compliant children will need extra encouragement do to their own thinking and to speak up for themselves. Because of a compliant child's lack of resistance, parents can step in to think and speak on behalf of their child, discouraging assertiveness. If compliant children are programmed by parents to be pleasers, they will not develop the sense of independence necessary for success and happiness. Our other son exhibited a somewhat compliant personality, in contrast to his brother, and, although we never saw signs of people-pleasing habits, we made a point of encouraging him to speak up for himself. Today, he, too, is adept at asserting himself.

Parents must see the big picture when it comes to instilling this trait in developing children. To continue the gardening metaphor, skillful assertiveness is one of the fruits of years of good parental cultivating. The seeds of self-acceptance, independent thinking, and conscious feeling lay the groundwork for assertiveness. If children have been discouraged from trusting themselves and what they think and feel, how could they possibly be equipped to stand up for themselves with confidence?

I encounter parents in my practice who, although they wouldn't admit it, subscribe to the old adage: children should be seen and not heard. These parents consider a child's protest, questioning, disagreement, expressed frustration and anger, even counter proposals all under the umbrella of "backtalk." Children of these parents aren't permitted to utter even a peep during a confrontation. I encourage parents to expect their children to express themselves properly, but shutting them down completely in conflict squanders a perfect teaching moment. Working through conflicts with children allows parents the opportunity to teach how to effectively express thoughts, feelings, and desires. Usually, children are more cooperative in conflict when they're allowed to express themselves than when they don't feel heard. Our sons were allowed to disagree with us and to be angry, so long as their thoughts and feelings were not expressed disrespectfully.

I've observed a range of communication patterns among parents and their children. I am heartened by the parents who encourage their children to speak for themselves and patiently listen until their children are finished expressing themselves. These parents tend to listen with the purpose of understanding and validating their child's thoughts and feelings. They apply active listening skills with children – perhaps the most effective way to plant the seeds of assertive communication. Active listening sends the message, "You have important and valid thoughts and feelings that are worthy of expression." Cultivating this belief in children is the key to their ability to assert themselves in the future.

These are also the parents who encourage their children to make developmentally appropriate choices and decisions for themselves. Something as simple as encouraging children to choose from a restaurant menu and place their own order is a practice in assertiveness, as is coaching a child to ask for help from teachers when needed, rather than rushing to the rescue. In fact, teaching your child to ask for help is probably one of the most important assertiveness skills we can teach. Explain to your child that admitting the need for help, and asking for it, are measures of strength and courage, not weakness.

Many parents I counsel are guilty of neglecting to plant the seeds of assertiveness in their children. These parents fail to listen to, understand, and validate their children's thoughts and feelings. Instead, they tend to dominate conversation, lecture, and speak for their children. Likewise, they over-protect, rescue, and make too many choices for their children, which deprives them of important learning experiences and opportunities to practice skills of assertiveness.

Children and teens also need some basic instruction in the mechanics of assertiveness relating to body language, eye contact, facial expression, and tone of voice. It was both striking and saddening, throughout my work with foster children, how few of those teenagers knew how to stand up straight, look someone in the eye, and introduce themselves. How could they possibly succeed in life if they don't know how to present themselves confidently? The field of child welfare has had to reckon with the fact that too many foster children leave care unprepared for independence, in large part due to their lack of interpersonal and other key life skills. Thankfully, some organizations have responded to this need by implementing life skills training courses, but more awareness and action are still needed.

And foster children are not the only ones at risk. All children need encouragement and guidance to communicate assertively. One of the many benefits of part-time jobs for teenagers is the invaluable learning experienced throughout the job search process. For example, the application stage gives parents the perfect opportunity to coach teens to present themselves assertively in an interview.

Parent-child conflict, although stressful, represents rich curriculum for teaching a child to communicate assertively rather than defensively and even how to negotiate. There were times in conflict with our sons when I would look for compromise if they were making a valid point and the effort to speak respectfully. And speaking of negotiation, I once took one of our sons, who was sixteen at the time, along with me to purchase a new car, knowing I'd have to negotiate assertively. I wanted him to witness it. When parents are alert to teaching these skills, the opportunities are abundant.

The following is a short list of incremental skills that comprise assertiveness. Look for everyday opportunities to guide your child in practicing them.

- Expressing thoughts and feelings directly
- Using an array of words that accurately describe feelings
- Applying non-verbal awareness (body language, eye contact, tone of voice)
- Stating a preference or an opinion
- Asking a question
- Asking for help
- Making a specific request
- Negotiating or making a proposal
- Saying no
- Explaining the reasons behind thoughts and feelings
- Making a complaint

Each day in the life of your child presents opportunities to teach one of these incremental skills, so long as you have the consciousness to recognize it. The immature parent is oblivious; the adult in the room sees the opportunities. Never lose sight of the fact that your children's success and happiness will rely in part on their ability to be assertive.

Sacrifice Applied to Parenting

I balance making sacrifices to meet the needs of my child and taking care of myself.

J ustin pulled into his driveway, turned the ignition off, and sat in his car for a minute to collect himself. It had been a stressful day at work and he wanted nothing more than to go inside, grab a cold beer, settle into his recliner, turn on Monday Night Football, and vegetate in front of the television for the rest of the evening. Justin knew, however, that on the other side of his front door were two young children anxious for every ounce of his attention and a wife eagerly anticipating some relief. Justin recited the pep talk he frequently has with himself. He reminded himself family was his highest priority and meeting the needs of his children will pay high dividends for them and his relationship with them and his wife. He recalled the words of a mentor who advised him to enjoy his kids while he can, because they'll be grown and gone before he knows it. He then reminded himself that this is what he signed up for. Justin took a deep breath, put his day job behind him, and made the conscious decision to focus on the responsibility and opportunity awaiting him as he walked toward that front door.

I know that internal pep talk well. I had many of them while raising our sons. But there were also times when my inner child drowned out the adult voice. One of the many differences between a child and an adult is that the child makes an effort only when he feels like it, whereas the adult makes the necessary effort even when he doesn't feel like it.

Imagine that Justin did indeed grab his cold beer and camp in front of his television after work. Picture him barking at his children to be quiet and not bother him because he's had a hard day. If Justin made a habit of this behavior, and many parents do, the systematic effect on his children and their relationship would be damaging, with many ripple effects.

I still recall the pride I felt as a new father, but I learned quickly that to be a parent required more than just being a father. In fact, the true definition of "parent" is more verb than noun. Nothing can really prepare us for the sacrifice required for parenting. I referred earlier to maturational loss, the concept that each stage of life presents predictable losses and potential gains. The transition to parenthood is a dramatic example of how maturational loss plays out. When we are able to accept the loss of much of our freedom, time, sleep, energy, money, and play and are able to give ourselves to our children, we gain a deep joy from a unique and unmatched human bond. Parents who have the maturity to sublimate their own needs to make the necessary sacrifices reap long-term rewards. Those who can't see beyond their own needs and resist making sacrifices usually experience permanently strained or distant relationships with their children.

Historically, the matter of sacrifice has been more of an issue with fathers than with mothers. Men, for generations, have rationalized their hard work to provide financially for their children as their share of responsibility and sacrifice. And to be fair, being a good provider qualifies as an important form of sacrifice, but this antiquated mind-set ignores the emotional needs that all children have of their fathers. I stated earlier that in my observation "father issues" are at the top of the list of grievances among my clients, with "mother issues" a close second. This is understandable, since many men are not wired for nurturing. Therefore, the average father has to consciously choose the work of nurturing to tap the most meaningful levels of sacrifice. Taking time and energy to nurture and teach is how the true bond between parent and child is formed. Rocking your child to sleep, changing diapers, giving baths, feeding, reading at bedtime, playing, helping with homework, teaching a skill, shuttling to and from activities, providing discipline – every minute and ounce of energy spent here are investments in your child's human potential and your priceless and indelible bond.

I can look back now and laugh at what exasperated me when our sons were growing up:

- The lack of peace, quiet, and relaxation in the evenings
- Endless messes and clutter
- The rare date night interrupted by a babysitter's call for help
- The end of weekend getaways
- Sleepless nights
- Less time for friends
- Forgetting how to discuss topics unrelated to children
- Very little spontaneity (at least the good kind!)
- Paying the babysitter
- Mealtime stress
- Lugging child paraphernalia everywhere
- Frequent bathroom stops on family trips
- Temper tantrums
- Giving up most weekend golf
- Bedtime battles
- Getting-ready-for-school and church battles
- Homework battles
- Sibling battles
- Disciplining your children while driving
- The constant shuttling from one event to another
- A sick child bringing life to a halt
- Contracting most of your child's illnesses
- Less spontaneous sex
- Less energy for even unspontaneous sex
- The cost of everything

- The stress of feeling every bit of physical and emotional pain your child experiences
- The guilt of over-reacting and losing control
- The weight of responsibility and worry from wondering how things will turn out

Before I discourage prospective parents, I can also say, without hesitation, the experience of those "in the thick of it" parenting years provided me deep joy and satisfaction and the ground for my most valued personal growth. The relationships we have with our sons will continue to bring us great joy for the rest of our lives. Had I understood this truth on a gut level when I was younger, I would have practiced more patience and acceptance. I would have had a deeper appreciation for the whole experience, including those exasperating moments, because I would have been more aware that the reward would make it all worthwhile.

As I write this, I'm acutely aware that I've been referring to typical types of parental sacrifices. I'd be remiss if I were to overlook those parents who make extraordinary sacrifices everyday due to the special needs of their children or the difficult circumstances in their lives. I have great respect and compassion for parents who are caring for children with chronic, debilitating diseases, children with physical and mental disabilities, learning disabilities, Asperger's Syndrome, or Autism, along with parents who adopt or provide foster care for abused and neglected children, and parents who have to work two jobs to sufficiently provide for their children. These parents make heroic sacrifices and we'd all do well to remember them when we complain about the trivial sacrifices required on the typical level.

In applying the adult trait of sacrifice to parenting, I must again emphasize the importance of balance. There are unhealthy versions of sacrifice in parenting. Just as there can exist too little sacrificing for your children, there can also be too much. When parents lose touch with their own needs and fail to tend to their own happiness and well-being, the negative effects ultimately impact their children. There are exceptions to all the rules, but in general, mothers are more at risk on this issue. Too often, I see a mother's chronic low-grade anxiety and depression darken day-to-day family life. The strong and wonderful nurturing trait in women can also make them predisposed to assuming a caretaker role that can run amok. The distorted version of caretaking can give parents the sense they're responsible for the well-being and happiness of everyone they love, particularly their children. They can worry constantly about the bad things that can happen and what they must do to prevent them. This distorted version of caregiving can lead parents to live on high alert, always anticipating the worst. If their children have problems, are unhappy, or struggle in some way, they blame themselves and rush to the rescue. This sense of responsibility for all the outcomes compels these parents to enable, protect, and control too much. Insidiously, while they are busy burning themselves out, assuming this overwhelming sense of responsibility for their children, they lose contact with who they are and their own valid needs, apart from their children. The longer they live this way the more depressed, anxious, and resentful they can become.

Our children need us to take good care of ourselves, in order for them to live with emotionally well-balanced and generally happy parents. They depend on us to radiate positive energy on most days. In order to supply them that energy, we must have ways of recharging our own batteries. There are times when it's absolutely appropriate to make your own needs the priority over the wishes of your children. This teaches your children healthy boundaries and prevents dependencies. It also models for them how to practice healthy self-care and create balance in their own lives.

I wince when parents tell me, sometimes with pride, that they've never spent a night away from their five year-old, or that they never leave their kids with a baby-sitter. I've seen homeschooling unconsciously driven by the co-dependency between parent and child. It's a red flag when parents can't identify an activity they do for fun or relaxation, are socially isolated or rarely spend time with friends apart from children, or can't talk about anything other than children. I'm also concerned when a couple can't specify what they do to nurture their relationship apart from children.

If you identify with the unhealthy version of caretaking or with these red flags, then you are likely already out of balance or soon will be. There are natural laws to life; the principle of balance is one of them. If you violate this natural law for long, you will do yourself and those closest to you harm. Nowhere is the principle of balance more important than in parenting.

When I reflect on my child-rearing years, I realize that period was, in many ways, "the best of times and worst of times." The experience could be at once both intensely stressful and joyous. Maturity, consciousness, and proactivity are required to strike that delicate balance between giving yourself to your children and taking good care of yourself. The stresses of child-rearing can challenge the most mature among us to override our instinct to avoid making necessary sacrifices. On the other side of the coin are those parents who aren't in touch with their own needs and at risk of sacrificing themselves to the point of neglecting their own well-being. There is a learning curve to finding this balance. The parents who can lay claim to giving themselves to their children and taking care of themselves are the happiest, healthiest, and most effective. These parents are the adults in the room.

Competence Applied to Parenting

I am cultivating a sense of competence in my child.

The core belief, "I am capable," is an essential building block for a positive sense of self. In some cases, children's capabilities seem to emerge almost in spite of the conditions in their environment, but those cases are the exceptions. As a rule, the competencies we want our children to eventually possess must be cultivated. Mature parents see the big picture and understand that every day in the life of a child represents potential curriculum. These parents recognize and seize the opportunities to convert daily experiences into teaching moments and life lessons in order to cultivate their child's skill development. They provide a range of experiences to enhance learning and to discover their child's innate abilities.

I've contracted with a local university for many years. This experience has involved countless hours of intense clinical work with college students and has given me a front row seat to observe the developmental transition from late adolescence to early adulthood. By now, with each new school year, I can predict what the most common themes will be with students. Since leaving home for college represents a major test of anyone's level of maturity and independence, I can anticipate that at the heart of many students' issues will be an exposed immaturity and a litany of dependencies.

Each year, students come to me reporting symptoms of high anxiety. In many cases, these students are overwhelmed by the responsibilities and social challenges of college life because they lack the skills required for independence. Typically, these students were either over-protected and micro-managed or not given enough guidance and support while growing up and now unconsciously carry a belief that tells them, "I can't deal with it." Some have never held a job, developed a work ethic, held a checking account, or managed their own money. Others have never experienced the level of responsibility required to organize and manage their time efficiently. Some have never participated in social groups or extra-curricular activities. Others haven't traveled or spent many nights away from home. Many previously succeeded academically by virtue of their innate intelligence, but lack the necessary study and organizational skills. Some are ignorant of the support resources available to students, much less the skill to ask for help and likewise, some are afraid to ask their professors for guidance. Yet, still others experience isolation for lack of social skills or the resourcefulness to find like-minded groups with which to be involved.

It's often the case that when students experience these feelings of incompetence, their fears and insecurities fuel high anxiety at the very time they need to take action and risks to gain competence. My experience counseling college-age students confirms that the degree to which children learn fundamental life skills has serious implications.

Yet another important lesson I picked up during my work with foster children was how much a child's skill development influences healthy growth. Because foster children often enter the system so skill-deficient, many foster care programs now utilize a life-skills assessment checklist to avoid the mistake of assuming these youth come with basic skills. I think every parent could benefit from a life-skill checklist; it's easy to assume children know how to do things they've never actually been taught. Remember the insight that behavior reflects learning. Here are some of the categories on the Life-Skills checklists:

Tangible Skills

- Personal appearance and hygiene
- Shopping and caring for clothes
- Grocery shopping
- Basic cooking skills
- Healthy eating
- Budgeting
- Banking
- Personal health care
- Emergency health care
- Housekeeping and maintenance
- Accessing public transportation
- Basic auto maintenance
- Job-seeking skills
- Accessing information and resources

Intangible Skills

- Social: meeting, conversing with, listening to people
- Awareness of personal boundaries
- Planning
- Organizing
- Goal-Setting
- Managing and expressing feelings
- Seeking help
- Assertiveness
- Dealing with conflict
- Negotiation
- Decision-making
- Problem-solving

Parents generally assume far too much regarding what kids know how to do. If you find ways to teach your children these life-skills, you will be equipping them to believe they're capable of dealing with whatever they will face.

Another important principle to keep in mind is all children are gifted, and it's our job to help discover and develop those gifts. Think of it as treasure hunting. All of us, especially developing children, need to believe and feel we are good at something. We're all born with certain natural abilities. Some children's abilities stand out while others lay hidden or dormant. The mature parent understands this principle of giftedness in children and is ever on the lookout to spot clues for buried treasure.

The combination of Howard Gardner's concept that there are many types of human intelligence, Daniel Coleman's concept of emotional intelligence, and the natural abilities outlined by *The Highlands Ability Battery* substantially support the truth that we are all inherently gifted in some way. I have drawn from these frameworks to create a hybrid list of "intelligence/ability" categories that parents would do well to recognize and cultivate in their children. These include: musical, linguistic, organizational, kinesthetic/athletic, theoretical, creative, mathematical, mechanical, visual/spatial, design, social/emotional, and analytical/problem-solving. A child's I.Q. and school performance are limited and often misleading indicators of intelligence and ability. I strongly recommend *The Highlands Ability Battery* for high school seniors. I consider it the best natural ability assessment available. Everyone has a natural ability profile; the feedback from this assessment can reveal abilities test-takers didn't know they possessed. This is the kind of empowering insight we should all have about ourselves. Mature parents view their children with a kind of X-ray vision to spot the subtle evidence of these latent intelligences and abilities in order to affirm and cultivate them.

Catherine and I required our sons to participate in a range of activities as they were growing up – cub scouts, church youth groups, choir, piano lessons, sports teams, summer camps, part-time jobs, volunteer service work, etc. We knew these experiences would provide them invaluable life lessons that would serve their skill development. We also knew exposure to these activities would help them identify their true interests and abilities that we could then further cultivate. As expected, some of these activities fell by the wayside for lack of their interest or ability, while others were pursued. We relied heavily on life lessons to do the teaching, but we also did our share of instructing and modeling many of the skills. As a result, we witnessed their growing confidence to take initiative, face new situations, and overcome obstacles. When our sons left for college, they were well-equipped for the new challenges, and they thrived. There was ample evidence they both believed, "I am capable," and "I can deal with whatever I have to face."

Each year, I encounter more students arriving at college with anxiety problems. My opinion is that many of these young people have been over-protected, over-managed, and over-indulged. Although their parents' intentions are good, this type of parenting systematically undermines a young person's sense of competence and, hence, confidence to deal with life. Sometimes a little benign neglect – the kind that allows for life to do the teaching, children to fight their own battles, and the freedom to learn from their own mistakes – is exactly what is best. If children see their parents smooth everything out for them, jump in and rescue them, and wring their hands over them, the message comes through loud and clear: "Bad things are going to happen and you can't handle it."

Then, of course, in some cases, there is the elephant in the room: the parental model. A notable percentage of these anxious students are life-skill deficient because of the dysfunction in their families caused by their parents' skill deficiencies. How do parents who don't manage their own lives help equip children? There are good answers to this question that involve taking adult steps: (1) acknowledge your own deficiencies, (2) commit to learning and practicing new skills, and (3) mobilize the resources that can offer your child the learning experiences you're unable to provide. Sometimes the most powerful model a parent can exhibit for a child is how to take responsibility for weaknesses and make changes.

Remember, one of the most important parenting functions is teaching. Sometimes parents are so busy trying to control and do everything for their children they fail to think like a teacher and miss opportunities to promote their children's skill development. Take a few minutes to create a life-skill checklist and a few teaching strategies in order to heighten your consciousness regarding this crucial aspect of your role as a parent. If you regularly plant the seeds of skill development through modeling and instruction, your children will one day leave home believing they are capable of dealing with life's challenges – a most important core belief that equips them to be future adults in the room.

Personal Growth Applied to Parenting

I am committed to my own learning and growth as a parent,
and I instill in my child the confidence to take risks
in order to learn and grow.

From the vantage point of sixty plus years of hindsight, I can see life is a process of ongoing learning and growth. I now realize everything I've experienced has served this process, especially the tough times. It's also clear that parenthood has provided me my richest growth. Just as marriage is the process of learning how to love, so too is parenting – only times ten. If I could wave a magic wand, I would have us all fear less and trust life's processes more, especially parents. As long as we do our part to nurture and to teach, our children will outgrow most of the things that worry us about them. Of course, this is easiest to see in hindsight.

Catherine and I complemented each other as parents. She helped me learn to nurture, and I provided her with perspective. When I became a parent, I already had years of experience working with troubled foster children, which provided a big picture understanding of child development. I knew the difference between serious childhood problems and normal ones. Our sons presented their share of normal problems. In those moments when Catherine would question, "Where did we go wrong?", I was able to reassure her we weren't off track, but rather dealing with their personalities and where they were developmentally. At times, I was able to successfully shift the focus away from our fear, worry, anger, and guilt to conscious, insightful, and strategic approaches to their behavior. My work gave me the advantage of viewing our own sons with some helpful objectivity.

When we have the objectivity to see our children as works in progress, insight to explain their behavior, and an understanding of developmental stages, we're equipped to have realistic expectations, respond strategically, practice patience, and trust life more. So many children and teenagers, with serious struggles, blossom and thrive over time. I've also seen parents learn new insights and skills to turn family life in a whole new positive direction. Our human capacity to learn and grow never ceases to amaze me.

Andrea was a thirty-year-old single mother of an eleven-year-old son, Nick. She was nineteen when Nick was born. Andrea brought Nick to counseling because his behavior had become increasingly out of her control, and she was at a loss as to how to handle his tantrums. Whenever she told him no or expected him to do something he didn't want to do, he'd explode in a fit of anger. What was telling was Nick exhibited this behavior only with his mother.

Andrea had a history of codependent relationships with abusive men. Her lack of a sense of self and her own boundaries led to a symbiotic relationship with her son. She'd been unable to discipline Nick properly, and as he became older and bigger, he began to overpower her. Since Nick hadn't been held accountable, he was very immature for his age.

This wasn't a simple matter of instructing Andrea on how to discipline. She said she knew what she was supposed to do with Nick, but could not bear making him unhappy. Her need for his love and approval prevented her from standing her ground with Nick, as was true in all her relationships with men.

The good news was that Andrea was committed to her own personal growth along with becoming a better parent. Therapy helped her realize that her problem setting boundaries with her son was symptomatic of her larger pattern of codependency. As Andrea developed a stronger sense of self and needed Nick's approval less, she became a stronger parent. As she learned to validate herself and her own needs more, she was able to see clearly that Nick's disrespectful behavior toward her was unacceptable. This growth empowered her to implement the kind of discipline that Nick needed from her.

Andrea also had to learn, in therapy, effective behavior management strategies. She learned to set firm rules and expectations with Nick and to use logical consequences consistently in order to hold him accountable. By the time we ended the counseling process, Andrea had grown personally and was parenting more effectively, Nick's behavior had improved significantly, and they were both much happier. Andrea provides a striking example of how dramatically we can change course when we're committed to looking at ourselves and learning how to parent effectively.

I have, however, seen many parents whose dysfunctional parenting was at the root of the child's problems, but were too insecure and defensive to look inward for solutions. These parents deny their child's problems are symptomatic of the negative dynamics in their family system. They expect counseling to fix their child without requiring any change on their part. When mature parents bring their child to counseling, they assume they're part of the equation, that there is something they need to learn, and they are receptive to feedback and guidance. In most cases, a child's willingness to take responsibility and make changes is in direct proportion to the parents' willingness to look at themselves. There is no more powerful way to plant the seeds of learning and growth in your children than to model for them an openness to constructive feedback and the resolve to act on it. Parents who defend against looking at themselves model how to be closed to learning and growth.

I remember vividly a session I had with a sixteen year-old boy and his mother. The pair came to counseling because of the son's defiant behavior, in the eyes of the mom. The son had confided to me previously his anger toward his mother for her frequent temper tantrums and habit of harsh commands when she expected something from him. He acknowledged he had become defiant with her out of this anger. I coached him to explain rationally to his mother how he felt and why. I had hoped this session would help them understand each other better. When the time came for this conversation, I was impressed with how maturely the son expressed himself to his mother, but he wasn't allowed to finish before she reacted so defensively the session fell apart. She was appalled I would "take his side," as she put it. I witnessed in that moment the son was the adult and the mom was the child. I was saddened by her inability to look at herself and by the missed opportunity for her to model listening, self-awareness, and openness to change. She and her son never came back. She expected me to simply fix her son without requiring any change on her part. Unfortunately, I have presided over many of those kinds of sessions, though in most cases parents are able to acknowledge their responsibility to make changes.

Many parents are committed to new learning and growth, and they instill this trait in their children. Modeling plants many of the seeds for this trait, but there are also clear messages to offer children that modeling will reinforce. Here are a few of them:

- Go for it.
- You learn by taking healthy risks.
- Change is a learning experience.
- Problems are opportunities for learning.
- You have to take risks to get what you want.
- It's OK to make mistakes, as long as you learn from them.
- It's more important to try than to avoid failing.
- Successes are built on previous failures.
- It's a sign of strength and courage to admit weakness and to ask for help.

Successful people live by these mantras and live dynamic lives because they're not afraid to take healthy risks, can admit weakness, ask for help, and learn from their mistakes. Some parents, however, send messages that inhibit a child's learning and growth. These parents project their own fears and insecurities onto their children. Here are some of the, mostly unspoken, messages they give their children:

- Play it safe.
- Don't risk it.
- Bad things will happen.
- What will people think?
- Mistakes and problems will look bad.
- It has to be perfect or don't try.
- Avoid change.
- Failure must be avoided at all costs.
- Deny weaknesses and the need for help.
- Defend yourself.

I am, again, emphasizing the power of thoughts and beliefs and the influence parents have on a child's programming. The adults in the room not only consciously live by the first set of mantras, but also plant those seeds for learning and growth in their children.

You are reading this book because you're making an effort to learn and grow. Consider the timeless principles and practices this section on mature parenting raises, and apply them with your children. Use the following evaluation to assess how well you're fulfilling your role as a nurturer-teacher; identify your strengths and weaknesses. Where you need improvement, set a goal and a few specific steps. If you take this evaluation seriously, your willingness to look at yourself and your commitment to learning and growth makes you the adult in the room.

Since we are all flawed and imperfect, if you are honest, you will, no doubt, identify some areas needing improvement as a parent. Don't dwell on your shortcomings. Focus on the steps you can take going forward. Allow yourself to be a parent in progress. Give yourself credit for your strengths. Trust that simply studying this assessment will raise your consciousness and improve your parenting. Give yourself credit for making the effort to read this book in order to learn and grow as a parent. Finally, be patient with yourself.

Nurturing

- I create a physically and emotionally safe home and family environment.

    Rating: 1   2   3   4   5

    Goal:

    Specific step:

- I am responsive to my child's emotional needs for love, belonging, affirmation, encouragement, support, and empowerment.

    Rating: 1   2   3   4   5

    Goal:

    Specific step:

- I build closeness with my child through loving touch, positive interaction, and quality time together.

    Rating: 1   2   3   4   5

    Goal:

    Specific step:

- I listen with the purpose of understanding, validating, and empathizing with my child's thoughts and feelings.

  Rating: 1   2   3   4   5

  Goal:

  Specific step:

- I create an orderly home and family environment with consistent organization and routines.

  Rating: 1   2   3   4   5

  Goal:

  Specific step:

- I instill in my child fundamental self-acceptance.

  Rating: 1   2   3   4   5

  Goal:

  Specific step:

- I cultivate in my child independent thinking.

  Rating: 1   2   3   4   5

  Goal:

  Specific step:

- I use insight to best understand my child's needs and behavior.

  Rating: 1   2   3   4   5

  Goal:

  Specific step:

- I balance making the necessary sacrifices for the needs of my child and taking care of myself.

  Rating: 1   2   3   4   5

  Goal:

  Specific step:

Teaching

- I model for my child the ten traits of the adult.

  Rating: 1   2   3   4   5

  Goal:

  Specific step:

- I cultivate my child's ability to process and manage feelings consciously.

  Rating: 1   2   3   4   5

  Goal:

  Specific step:

- I instill in my child positive core beliefs about self, others, the future, and life in general.

    Rating: 1   2   3   4   5

    Goal:

    Specific step:

- I instill in my child a sense of personal responsibility and a strong work ethic.

    Rating: 1   2   3   4   5

    Goal:

    Specific step:

- I cultivate insight within my child.

    Rating: 1   2   3   4   5

    Goal:

    Specific step:

- I cultivate my child's ability to communicate assertively.

    Rating: 1   2   3   4   5

    Goal:

    Specific step:

- I instill in my child a strong sense of competence through the modeling and instructing of key life skills.

    Rating: 1   2   3   4   5

    Goal:

    Specific step:

- I discipline my child proactively and strategically with consistent rules and natural and logical consequences.

    Rating: 1   2   3   4   5

    Goal:

    Specific step:

- I provide a variety of play experiences for my child.

    Rating: 1   2   3   4   5

    Goal:

    Specific step:

- I instill in my child the value of taking risks for the purpose of learning and growth.

    Rating: 1   2   3   4   5

    Goal:

    Specific step:

A Closing Word

W hen I started the journey of writing this book, I had no way of knowing for sure where it would take me. Now I can see this process has been a metaphor for how our lives work at times. To reach this point, I've had to consciously apply many of the principles and practices addressed in these pages. This has been at once a humbling, frustrating, discouraging, and exhilarating process. Since my career allows for precious little spare time, I've worked on this in fits and starts and bits and pieces, often going back to re-work entire sections and constantly tweaking sentence structure and word use. I have a whole new appreciation and respect for writers. This process has required of me considerable patience and persistence – two more traits of adulthood.

I've had to maintain a steady vision of what I wanted to accomplish while life's distractions and stresses attempted to throw me off course and derail my focus. I've had to work through, at times, my insecurities as a writer by consciously practicing trust in who I am, what I think and believe, and what I've learned in my personal and professional life. I've had to practice consciously managing my feelings along with conscious and positive thinking to keep myself encouraged and, at times, to talk myself off the ledge, so to speak. I've had to remind myself to keep going, because it takes "10,000 hours" of practice to be good at something. I've had to repeatedly choose to risk failure by continuing to write with no indication of what the outcome might hold. I practiced focusing on my learning and growth during this process and began to recognize that writing was enhancing my clinical work, which took the pressure off the eventual success of this book. This meant there was no way I could fail. If this book never saw the light of day, the gains I was already experiencing was making it all worthwhile.

You can see where I'm going here. The conscious practice of these traits has sustained me through this endeavor and utterly confirms their relevance for me. This strengthens my conviction to encourage you to take to heart the practice of this book's ten adult traits – self-acceptance, independent thinking, personal responsibility, conscious feeling, positive core beliefs, insight, assertiveness, sacrifice, competence, and personal growth.

You're on your own unique journey. Where you find yourself today is where you're supposed to be, based on your level of consciousness. If you like where you are, then chances are this book has confirmed you're already on the right path and you're applying many of its principles and practices. If so, stay on the path.

If you don't like where you are, take heart. You can choose today to begin walking the path on which you want to travel as an individual, a spouse, a parent, or all three. It is never too late to change your trajectory. Everything in your past – your mistakes, failures, regrets, losses, and wounds – has the potential to be your curriculum and a source of your strength going forward. You can't grow, however, if you dwell on the negatives in yourself and in your past.

Since you've read this far, I have confidence that some important seeds for your growth and maturity have been planted. It'll be up to you, through the application of this book's principles and practices, to cultivate these seeds so they might bear fruit. I have no doubt that, regardless of where you are on your journey, if you practice these traits with patience and persistence through good times and bad, you will be sustained and will grow. Just be realistic about your expectations. Growth is slow, subtle, incremental – difficult to measure in the short run, but deeply rewarding in the long run.

Even with flaws, you are a divinely worthy and acceptable human being. You will always be a work in progress with the capacity to learn and grow. Practice living more consciously one day at a time and one small step at a time, and you will become the adult in the room.

Acknowledgments

I can't remember now what Rev. Cherie Larkin said in her message on that July Sunday morning of 2011. I know that whatever she said helped me decide to start writing as I walked to the car after the service. You never know when and from whom the right message will speak to you. Thank you, Rev. Larkin.

I also want to thank the people whose labor of love helped make this book possible. My wife Catherine has almost as much time invested in this as I do. She typed every word as well as all the edits and rewrites. She provided me invaluable feedback, and her support and encouragement helped keep me going at times.

My daughter-in-law, Beth Roberts Kelly, used her journalism background over countless hours to thoroughly edit and refine my manuscript. She, too, gave me invaluable feedback and encouragement as did four designated readers: Dr. Sheila Graham Smith, Dr. David Elkins, Dr. Jackie Palka, and Rod Williams, LCSW.

I owe so much to my parents, Louise and Earl Kelly, for providing me such a good foundation on which to build. I'm eternally grateful to our sons, Graham and John, for teaching me much about human growth and development and for their feedback and support in this book-writing process.

Finally, from the bottom of my heart I want to thank my clients for their courage to make themselves vulnerable with me and for their commitment to learning and growth. They have truly been my teachers and my inspiration.

CPSIA information can be obtained at www.ICGtesting.com
Printed in the USA
LVOW11s1704030815

448642LV00002B/454/P